The Poetry of Everyday Life

POETS ON POETRY

David Lehman, General Editor
Donald Hall, Founding Editor

New titles

John Hollander, *The Poetry of Everyday Life*
Geoffrey O'Brien, *Bardic Deadlines*

Recently published

Josephine Jacobsen, *The Instant of Knowing*
William Logan, *All the Rage*
Charles Simic, *Orphan Factory*
William Stafford, *Crossing Unmarked Snow*
Anne Stevenson, *Between the Iceberg and the Ship*
May Swenson, *Made with Words*
C. K. Williams, *Poetry and Consciousness*

Also available are collections by

A. R. Ammons, Robert Bly, Philip Booth, Marianne Boruch,
Hayden Carruth, Fred Chappell, Amy Clampitt, Tom Clark,
Douglas Crase, Robert Creeley, Donald Davie, Peter Davison,
Tess Gallagher, Suzanne Gardinier, Allen Grossman, Thom Gunn,
John Haines, Donald Hall, Joy Harjo, Robert Hayden,
Daniel Hoffman, Jonathan Holden, Andrew Hudgins,
Weldon Kees, Galway Kinnell, Mary Kinzie, Kenneth Koch,
Richard Kostelanetz, Maxine Kumin, Martin Lammon (editor),
David Lehman, Philip Levine, John Logan, William Matthews,
William Meredith, Jane Miller, Carol Muske, John Frederick Nims,
Gregory Orr, Alicia Ostriker, Marge Piercy, Anne Sexton,
Charles Simic, Louis Simpson, William Stafford,
Richard Tillinghast, Diane Wakoski, Alan Williamson,
Charles Wright, and James Wright

John Hollander

The Poetry of
Everyday Life

Ann Arbor

THE UNIVERSITY OF MICHIGAN PRESS

2001   2000   1999   1998   4   3   2   1

A CIP catalog record for this book is available from the British Library.

Library of Congress Cataloging-in-Publication Data

Hollander, John.
    The poetry of everyday life / John Hollander.
        p.   cm.—(Poets on poetry)
    ISBN 0-472-09684-2 (acid-free paper). — ISBN 0-472-06684-6
(pbk. : acid-free paper)
    1. Hollander, John—Authorship.   2. Poetry.   I. Title.
II. Series.
PS3515.03485P55   1999
811'.54—dc21
                                                        98-39034
                                                           CIP

To Rosanna Warren

Contents

Introduction

I was brought up in that atmosphere of high modernism which discouraged one from talking about oneself and inflicting unwanted autobiographical material on readers. Believing that my poetry would do so figuratively and perhaps more profoundly, I still remain somewhat reticent in the old way to discuss what I have written, or how, or why. But the fact of this little volume, and its somewhat peculiar shape, seem to call for a bit of explanation.

Milton spoke of his prose as having been written with the left hand, and yet, given that formidable body of work, one feels that he had two right ones. Dryden, Emerson, Arnold, Eliot were all ambidextrous in an exemplary way. With considerably more modesty, I might myself think of the scholarly publication I've done as being the work of my left hand; but a good deal of my critical and interpretive prose has been written more by the right hand than the left, as a poet and not as a university scholar. Some of this work is collected here.

I notice now that only about a quarter of the literary criticism I have written in the form of reviews or review-essays (including many brief monthly ones for *Harper's* in the early seventies) concerned contemporary poetry. Some have been republished in my books of "scholarly" studies, but there are several of another sort that I have wanted to reprint outside of any academic context. They were conceived without footnotes, and were directed toward a general reader rather than a professionalized academic audience. And I acknowledge that this is despite the fact that, during the past forty years, more and more readers of poetry have been concentrated in the academy. Yet I have come to the unhappy conclusion that there are and will continue to be fewer and fewer professors of English who know what a poem is and how to read and teach others to read it. In any case, this book is addressed to readers of poetry of any persuasion.

As a later-twentieth-century writer who attended college in the aftermath of World War II, I encountered (at Columbia then, in particular) a way of life that was both academic and literary rather than scholarly and, perhaps, in an older premodernist way, belletristic. I began to hear a vocation for college teaching during the same years in which I felt some imperatives from the voice of poetry. Partially because of a generation of teachers of my own (Mark Van Doren, Lionel Trilling directly; Robert Penn Warren, John Crowe Ransom, Allen Tate, John Berryman indirectly) I could conceive of myself as being a university teacher and a poet in the way that Williams and Stevens and Eliot were doctor or lawyer or bank clerk or publisher and poet. (Not, I might add, as a poet making a somewhat grudging living teaching creative writing, but as a literary scholar and critic.) It must be said that I was lucky enough to be a professor of English at American universities during what may have been a uniquely privileged moment—the roughly thirty years from 1960 to 1990. During this period, someone well read and of a thoughtful turn of mind might well have chosen to become—after some professional training of varied quality, point, and utility—a teacher of literature. It was a way of continuing to explore and rethink and contrive new ways of explaining—to oneself as well as to students—in the very activity of teaching, which can often be closer to poetic process than might at first be thought.

Analogously, I now perceive in the interpretive pieces in this volume a teacherly impulse. As criticism, they tend to explain and explore rather than to propound judgments. All of the writing I have been fortunate enough to be able to collect in this volume was done, with one early exception, over the past fifteen years or so. These pieces are of several sorts. Some are poetic fictions in prose (not, in fact, prose poems, but rather parabolic or otherwise enigmatic narratives); some are considerations, several quite informal, of the work of other poets among my contemporaries; there are two memorials, of very different kinds, to poets I have known and profoundly admired; there are some observations on the eternal problem of verse translation; and there is one of a good number of interviews I have given over the years, selected because it is one of the three I felt I most learned from and, in this case, the most recent. I hope that the whole will have the organized variety and the savor of an ongoing pot-au-feu rather than the faint aroma of an otherwise desiccated potpourri.

The Poetry of Everyday Life

> The finest poetry was first experience; but the thought has
> suffered a transformation since it was an experience.
> Cultivated men often attain a good degree of skill in writing
> verses; but it is easy to read, through their poems, their
> personal history: any one acquainted with the parties can
> name every figure; this is Andrew and that is Rachel. The
> sense thus remains prosaic. It is a caterpillar with wings, and
> not yet a butterfly. In the poet's mind the fact has gone
> quite over into the new element of thought, and has lost all
> that is exuvial.
>
> —Emerson, "Shakespeare; or, The Poet"

I hope that my title is not too misleading, and this is just to say
that by "the poetry of everyday life" I do not mean casual verses of
the sort that W. C. Williams tacked up on the refrigerator door to
explain the missing plums. (Mrs. Williams's longing might have
been filled by a trope of the eaten fruit; Dr. Williams's excuse
could never flower, in this case, into true poetry, but only litera-
ture.) That genre is indeed a common one, and no discussion of
contemporary poetry could fail to remark upon it. Such critical
discussions are concerned with poetry as literature—the current,
the received, the fashionable—and I hope that in my concern for
poetry I can't be faulted for slighting literature, as an institution
involving readers, journals, producers of printed commodities,
styles, modes, and so forth. But here I'll forbear to discuss the
everyday life of poetry in America—the secular religiosity that
has overcome the production and reception of banal verse; the
religiosity with which any printout with an unjustified right-hand
edge is sanctified as poetry; the fashions—formal, gestural,
ideological—into which falls the stuff, not of fiction or poetry,
but of literary verse today.

Published in *Raritan* 1 (fall 1981).

The "everyday life" of my title does not mean the contemporary quotidian, the world of the new and the news that is discourse about it. Even discourse can, under some circumstances, prove exciting and valuable. For me, I'm afraid that now is not such a time. "It does not appear unthinkable," writes the American philosopher Stanley Cavell in a book that should mean as much for poets as for epistemologists—"It does not appear unthinkable that the bulk of an entire culture, the culture thinking aloud about itself, hence believing itself to be talking philosophy, should become ungovernably inane. In such a case you would not say that the Emperor has no clothes; in part because what you really want to say is that there is no Emperor; but in greater part because in neither case would anyone understand you." So I shall forsake the world of emperors and subjects of that sort; my "everyday" is not "today" necessarily, but only for example.

Some of the questions criticism has been invited to address have concerned "today necessarily." What is of the day is journalism, and much literature is indeed that. The sociology of style—of what is called "form" in poetry—is itself interesting journalism about journalism, and I shall remark more than once on how literature, in speaking for itself, prefers to answer the questions of a gossip columnist rather than those of a political theorist, as it were. The gossip is usually about feeling, or about form; it is never about meaning, or about imagination, or about thought and trope, and it seldom considers—out of *pudeur* and terror—the great poetry of the past unless it has been scaled down in representation, and weakened into hearsay.

But even though it is late in the spring, and my dooryard is as yet unraked of last winter's leaves, I shall forgo the clearing away of the debris of last season's inane discourse to dig at one corner of the lawn, down to the heart of the matter. Analyzing the relations of journalism, religion, modernism's role in the formation of literary canons and college curricula, the rise and spread of inept free verse as the contemporary American replacement of inept rhymed jingle (even as an easy rusty irony has displaced an earlier sentimentality), the cultural politics of vulgarity generally—I shall attend to all this later. (And I must do it myself: there is no hiring of earnest students to do this work any more—even at outrageous wages—for none have been taught to know leaves or to hold a rake at the right angle.) For now, I shall dig at the poetry itself.

"The subject of a poem," said Hobbes, "is the manners of men, not natural causes." But the manners of men, and of women, is what contemporary verse, for all its mythological gestures and clichéd figures of pathos, is all about. We should rather reply to Hobbes that it is what lies between "the manners of men" and the "natural causes"—connecting, mediating, mutually transforming them—that is both the subject and object of poetry. All the rest is literature, as Verlaine declared after having insisted that poetry was music before all else—a symbolist song about poetry being trope before all else. In "the poetry of everyday life" we can take "of" in the sense of "about" or "on the subject of," and the whole phrase to denote some of this literature, reportage, versified journalism. But poetry is a matter of figuration; and I have made "of" in "the poetry of everyday life" to be genitive and attributive. In my phrase, I denote the poetry that everyday life *is,* rather than providing little topics and themes for.

The literature of everyday life renews itself eternally. But the poetry is another matter; and the notion of a poetry free of literature—liberated from the bondage with which it goes the dreariest and the longest journey—is on the face of it puzzling. Even a notebook page is public; samizdat is a journalistic tradition; the idea of a theater, as Francis Fergusson first showed us, inheres in every instance of A doing a routine for, or even a domestic number on, B. What can I in particular—whose concern for the text rather than the throwaway may have become evident by now—mean by what appears to be a textless poetry?

Were I to have invoked the Poetry of Everynight Life, I might be immediately understood to mean dreaming, which, in possibly the greatest piece of poetic criticism of our age, Freud redeemed from fancy, for the imagination, from frivolity and insignificance, for truth. He did this by taking dreams as seriously as if they were important poems; the result has been, among other things, to allow us to compare poems to dreams once more without being silly thereby, and without thereby refusing to consider seriously everything about poetry that was intentional, and carefully constructed—intention and structure being those elements that most general, pre-Freudian senses of *dream,* once common sense had purged it of the notion of prophecy, had ignored.

On the other hand, if I now began to discuss what used to be called "daydreaming," you would have a right to feel cheated: it would be an evasion of a commitment to my insistence that the stuff of poetry is meaning, woven on a warp of significance, a weft of design.

In order more immediately, then, to distinguish the literature *about* daily life from the poetry *of* it, let's now proceed to a number of examples of this poetry, and to some procedures for discerning it, momentarily free of its usual envelope, carapace, costume, or whatever formal or casual literary duds.

Talking to Our Cats It is their very independence of us, their mythical self-sufficiency, that makes them so malleable, like language itself. They do not possess, but rather *are*, a kind of language, and one is always taking cats figuratively. We interpret them when we address, and then respond to, their silences, whereas we merely come to understand, without intervening fables, models, or metaphors, our dogs. Cats are named differently from dogs, not in that *Fido, Rags,* or *Spot* would be inappropriate (there are cats so named, cats who have been made clowns), but because feline names are never in a true grammatical vocative. Cats never respond to their *names* per se, as do dogs. Their names are the titles of poetic texts, the names of tropes, into which all of the uncharacterizable life of each particular cat seems to grow. We read the cat as we do an unfolding book, and our glossing of its invisible expressions is like moralizing a dark, pregnant myth. Our discourse is with a fable we have invented, albeit in order to explain one of the most compelling of presences, a domestic spirit. Its response to us, and ours to it, are both parts of a parable.

The Eternal Mutual Impingements of the Weather and Our Consciousness of It That consciousness may or may not include a recognition of the traditional, proverbial givens of such impingements—the willowy arch of the long hair of the weeping girl, the rain falling in the heart of the rueful town. Reading the text of the book of daily life, in which the weather—and the separate sense we have of ourselves as living in its domain—are both major fictions, whether of person or of place: this is itself to write a new book. Which same may be heroic, as when we seem to be subjects of the weathery kingdom, living under the reign of a sunless king, or, in a later age, moving in the republic of our own sunlight. The force with which a fine day confirms our elation or mocks our despair is the same one with which a starry night causes even a caressing hand to shiver, or opens up the heavy atlas of understanding. There is no end to this mutual rereading, ours of the unending emblem of the weather, of the mysterious high- and low-pressure areas in ourselves.

Revelations of the Priority of Meaning —And how American this is! We, whose surrounding waters were Lethean, who dwell among effacements of where we have been, must always feel that origins are secondary, are derived, and that what has descended from them is primary rather, and thereby prior. Our forebears are rooted in ourselves, trace back to us, and blossom in our chronicles as well-made artificial flowers. Our common words originally came into the world as embodiments of our uses of them; the belated fables composed by etymologists are charming and compelling, but they come into the world so many ages after the fact of our experience. *Silly* means "silly," which we know well in childhood: the assertion that it once meant "innocent" and before that, "blessed" and "lucky," is the derivative, ironic epigram stretched by a modern poet to cast a shadow across our sophistication. This is what we feel we know, living in the world of our words. But then we are translated.

Long ago, musing on the shores of childhood, I considered the names of my friends and classmates; the more I read and heard of, the more I wondered that so many English families of the past should have acquired what were so obviously, and originally, American boys' first names—Herbert, Howard; Irving, Milton, Morris; Russell, Sidney; Wayne and Dwight—as surnames. New priorities seemed to arise. What dawned was not merely more light but, each morning, a few more degrees of horizon reaching around behind my ears until I could hear the echoes of history, and learn how, in the matter of names, it was the new discoveries that came first. And so with all the other words, aside from proper names. And so with the unending

tournament of the two champions of a word's "real" meaning—
What it Means locked in shadowy combat with What it Once
Meant. *Clear* and *obscure* contend with their semantic ancestors,
radiance and darkness. Once we have tripped over some pave-
ment of meaning and learned of their mental fight, we have
changed for the world as much as it has for us, and neither can
ever get together in quite the same way any more.

The Wonder, Not at the Matter of Being, But at How Questions of Being
Explode into Galaxies of Other Matter   —Becoming, that is, ques-
tions of being this or that; when or then; here now in a midnight
field of high stubble reaching into the star-flawed darkness of
summer sky, or there, then, in the artificial light of the figura-
tive kindergarten, seriously pasting a gold star on blue paper.
And of being in the world of multiplicities of modes of worldli-
ness, those that shape the meanings of "being," those that cause
the sky and the paper to bend toward each other and with
extended hands to exchange the gifts of resemblance.

The Marriage of the Wandering Mind to the Attentive One   The wed-
ding was a secret, and neither wears a ring. The partners are
generally known separately, and both are ordinary candidates
for representative in the unacknowledged legislature. The Wan-
derer? He who drops the scrubbing brush from unhurried fin-
gers into the soapy kettle, and stares out into acres of virtual
space, as a strong-winged irrelevancy of far delight or near loss
comes homing across the fields at him. Or who drops his hur-
ried fingers from the keyboard, vacating the place of labor that
there may be space for flight. The Attentive One? She who
cleaves to the loom, making up her mind in a fabric of figura-
tions that draws the world into place around her. Or she who
perceives the shaded lowliness of the mushrooms in their som-
breros, flicking it into focus with the brush of phrase. We have
heard much of both of them, but it is their marriage in us that
we usually fail to acknowledge, but that can overcome us with
moments of its domesticity. That is when the Task and the De-
sire, momentarily wearied of hounding each other, of dodging
the flung pots and pans, sink into a wide bed, canopied with
figures accepted from the streetlamps through drawn shades.

Consider the Space You Inhabit When You Can See Nothing Lie in the sun, suspended, preferably, by a deck chair, lest the curving hardness of ground, the scratching of grass against your back, be too touching a reminder of all that earth, the horizontality of death, the vulnerability of our surfaces, has come to mean. Inhabit for a while, instead, another region of bodily experience: let the heat of the sun on your closed eyes and left shoulder blend in a most painterly fashion with the faint, cool breeze leaking out of the stand of invisible trees over your right shoulder. (If you cry out for color, smell the tincture of mown grass in it, then.) This is the checkered shade of paradise. Not the ruled squares of light and dark, into each of which we run seeking relief from the eventual tyranny of the other, but the experience of heat and shade as themselves and as phases of something major, meeting in a zone of indeterminacy halfway across your chest.

There is no room for the eye here. The space of your world is more enclosed than the contingent openness into which our eyes keep finding, and poking, holes. But it extends across the front of us, it is shaped to fit the delicate landscape of our own curvature, whereas the eye's just but unimaginative compass traces out its horizontal circle around us with such unfailing constancy that we trust it to have completed the task always behind our backs. The rest of the circle is always there, and we do not, in fact, jut out of some flat background; space does not terminate behind us, but this is only what we have had to come to believe. The dog's space is not that of his eye, and what he sees are only appearances screened and distanced by his skepticism. His nose invites and confirms his knowing, whereas for us scent is a chink in our walls, a spyhole open to rumor, hint, and, of course, memory. The dog's space of awareness extends 360 degrees around him, and smelling is as seeing through a band of eyes encircling his whole frame. Thus it is not a matter of trust for him that he inhabits the center of his room. He knows that he does; whereas we know too much else of and about ourselves in the world, let alone too much and too little about knowing itself. We know that we are not centers but trivial epicenters; that all of the Emersonian circles we make and inhabit crowd available space and, intersected and overlaid like far too many engraved lines, create a cosmos of murk; that our eyes are all fussy landscape painters after all, academic in their systems of illusion, derivative and anxious in their allusiveness to various kinds of picture. All this we know from scholarly works in the same library on inference whose children's reference room reassures that our 120 degrees of visible arc is completed behind us.

Your eyes have opened, now, onto the painting before you. Near greens, both yellowed by sunlight and darkened, move off into layers of distance, through archways cut among dark pines, into further layers. The painter has colored the distant spruces blue, and the gouache at your feet gives way to the wash of the farthest hills. But return for a moment to the near but far from spherical space of the heat and the cool: your own sweat and the rising breeze have altered the way it contains you, yet it remains the same realm of total knowledge of our world. If a bee stings now, or a backache seizes, it goes to show how shattery, how fragile that realm is. But unfractured, the skin's profoundest grasp of space itself reigns supreme, and perspective, inference, extrapolation, puzzlement, and wonder lie rusted against the garden wall, like outgrown perambulators, seesaws, and swings, like wheelchairs, crutches, and leg-braces for cripples long since healed.

The Riddle of the Sphinx   It is a mistake to think that this was a question that had been formerly posed to a finite series of travelers ending with the Correct Answerer. Not to realize that we must continue to try to answer it is the mistake we all continue to make. The Riddle of the Sphinx is the Sphinx herself; her apparent historical and formal existence is a trap; her continuing presence is like the puns we overlook in a conundrum, the alternative we reject in a solution or proof, only to wail or snarl when it is pointed out to us later as the right path we refused to take. For she is always here, now, with us, lurking in puzzling and ambiguous reflections on water or in windows we pass, inhering in double-exposed photographs or staring out of areas of erasure in uncompleted drawings.

You may see her even in the apparently unambiguous representations, the ones we should least expect her to inhabit. An academy painting glistening with the inauthenticity of its high finish, actually purporting to show her in the original scene— she will in fact be there, at least once, for each of us. Consider

such a painting: the famous crossroads, framed by unremark-
able hills untransformed even by the strangely whitened but
sunless sky, the kind of daylight that gives the air some of the
density of night, revealing everything as if momentarily, as if all
vision were about to be withdrawn. The light of showdowns. And
there, frightful in the cheesy frightfulness of her form, as in the
certain violence of her action should we fail, making an obscen-
ity of our very canniness, she sits in a bad picture, putting forth
her riddle with the same old answer: "What are the Astonishing
and the nauseatingly Ordinary both examples of?"

Learn to Inspect the Snapshots of Our Attention   It is only by misread-
ing those discrete moments of vision for their apparent continu-
ity that the illusion of motion can occur, with its consequent
frauds of the quotidian, its lies of the ordinary. These snapshots
are not the grotesque freeze-frames plucked out of movie film,
presenting pictures we never see at all (and yet, we are shocked
to observe, are part of what we have been seeing); these snap-
shots are those unposed, unarranged pictures that become em-
blems of our consciousness. Consider, for example:

You rush down a corridor, message in hand, turn into a
room, and behold from the side a young woman, stark naked,
standing in a shallow, rectangular puddle of sunlight, down at
which she gazes as if in meditation, off toward the right. Her
skin is winter pale, her long, dark hair falls halfway down her
back, and her left hand is extended, slightly curved and palm
downward. You immediately frame snapshots of surprise and
desire; but these are soon followed by other, broader and more
complex pictures. Down the room, to your right, is the artist,
working away at his reddish clay. It appears that you have not
"caught" the girl in a moment of meditation, after all; she has
rather caught you in a moment of extrapolated astonishment,
and even as your heart beats wildly for a moment in wonder and
then warmth, you are turned to a kind of stone by the click of
her shutter. She is not a person being herself, espied in a mo-
ment of contemplation of something beyond her—the pool of
sunlight obstructing the window on the floor—that is yet her-
self. No: she is a model; she stands for—as one may be said to
"sit for"—the artist. His finished piece will stand for her as well,
but in another sense, a way that recircles the meanings, and

even the priorities, of object and image. She stands for the modeling process, which will produce an image that will stand for her. And yet even here the two senses of the phrase are again reversed: the finished image will stand for the modeling of the girl's gaze, the gaze of a model who represents her image.

This is what you see in those later snapshots, those that take in the artist, the modeled figure growing in particularity through several successive phases, the changing rectangles of sunlight on the floor. They will, however, illustrate no dusty tales that one might tell of artists and models—such as that of the model who turned slowly to stone as her completed, carved figure came gradually alive; or of the model who felt each movement of the painter's brush along the surface of the unseen figure of herself on the canvas as a caress so passionate that she had to seize her body with her hands and give way to her own, not to the painter's, desire; or of the model who was literally consumed as her image grew—not bit by bit, fingers, toes, ears dissolving into the afternoon light, but in a reversed recapitulation of the act of modeling, losing detail and specificity, shrinking or ballooning into general form and, finally, into a huge lump of the stuff of earth; or of the model whose own work of art consisted of this séance: herself in this room with an artist (enacted by a friend), playing at representing something of her. For these tales one needs the illustrative hand of shadowy mezzotints and stilted engravings. The Fable your snapshots take up—perhaps attested to in legends scrawled lightly across their backs—is too large and open: the Fable of what goes on, the tale that interprets itself.

Keep them, for what it is that they are snapshots of will vanish, even as the snapshots themselves will vanish like now-unfrozen frames in an unreeling array. You cough. The artist looks up. The model complains of the cold and breaks her pose. You enter the room with paper in extended hand and say, "This came for you." The paper is taken, read, understood or misunderstood, as the case may be; and there are consequences of this. But they are black and blank, like the covers of the old album in which snapshots used to be kept, and speak of nothing but their closure.

Take One of the Forgotten Books That Has Been Propping Up One Corner of the Sagging Table, Dust It Off, and Read It Very well: here is an old, dusty volume—not very old, really, but certainly dated. *The Book of Airplanes.* Reading it is to ask, "What is the parable of the aircraft and our flight in it?" Flight is surely our contemporary version of the old moralists' road, The Way. Well, we may learn from the airplane

1. that dark clouds gleam brightly when seen from above;
2. that the fastest motion forward through the air is the least eventful;
3. that, one way or another, we will descend.

Consider the Young Person Kneeling over the Pond (Look at him, yes, with any of the particular desires—to touch and know, or to remember, or to organize available visual space with the curve of bending back, the face averted and hidden below the line of sight. Succumb to any of these if you will—call out a name, walk over and caress, turn away to look into the shade falling on the far lawn, reach for your sketchbook and pencil. Then go away. Now, the rest of you who are still here, consider the young person kneeling over the pond:) There are several schools of consideration, and it is well to know of them before falling into reflective depths oneself. One of these maintains that the young man is studying the pond—the slanting sunlight on the far surface, the agitation of wavelet nearby, the several depths of water, rock, and mud and the discursive weeds moving among them, the large, pausing fish and the minute, vanishing ones— and that not only is he therefore a serious person, but that he is being considered with seriousness.

Another view is that he studies nothing but his image in the water—knowing it to be an image only and something other than himself, mindful of old fables, but nonetheless (or perhaps all the more) absorbed in the half-presence that is on the water, or in it, or whatever. Such a view holds that there is nothing else to be seen anymore, and that if the young person claimed to be investigating the pond he would either be lying or, more likely, unwittingly frivolous. As frivolous, indeed, as the first school considers the second to be.

But our tales are told out of school, and our fables spring from their own antiquities. We are latecomers enough to this spot to realize that if he sees the pond—its shallows and its bottom, its room and the objects in it—he can only do so by looking down through the shadow of his own motionless, searching head. Only within the bounds of the cool darkness of its contemplative shade will the water's surface not defy any gaze with the derision of ripples, the laughter of returning sunlight that so charmingly parodies reflection, and turns it away. Only within that darkened frame will rock, fish, weed, and the silt below them rise slowly into perceptibility, as if the eye, breathing deeply, were slowly quickening.

Perhaps that is enough of a lesson, and those who have learned it—or have learned that, indeed, they knew it already— may leave. (There are so few of us left now that I might as well whisper—the truth is too perplexing and fragile to shout or even to proclaim.) Very well. Look at the water-gazer again: he does indeed see into and through and in and among the regions of water; he does, in fact, do so by means of his own reflection. But in this wise: he sees his image but does not, as in the previous interpretation, look through it. Rather, in the dim, mirrored versions of his eyes swimming in the dark green, he sees, magnified in their pupils, the whole realm that lies below, beyond, his image—lighter and darker darks; forms, shapes, stillnesses; algae and pebbles; a lost and rusted hook flying a whisp of line; and, deeper in the cold gray below, two sunken perch, fins barely breathing in the slow stream. All this is truly there, but there by means of the seer's own image, and by far different means from those offered by the happy accident of science we spoke of before, that allows a reflection to hold up a shading and elucidating hand to dazzled eyes.

But this will be impossible to explain to the two schools of fishing and Narcissus.

Confound the Rhetorician   Take his fussing, his distinctions, his protestations that the glories of what we see, the horrors of what we fear, the pleasures and the pains that touch us are all mere tropes. Take these with you on your morning walk into the country, and—No: do not throw them away, down into the first abyss you pass, or in the last metal garbage can provided by the town. For then the rhetorician will have confounded you: his trope will have been realized in your trash, and he will have won whatever combat you sought to wage between the troops of common sense and nonsense. No: take them with you, all his tools and toys, but take them seriously, more seriously, perhaps, than the rhetorician could.

I know what the antiquarians will now say: "Yes, yes: you, not the rhetorician, will find true language in the woods—run-on sentences in rivers, synecdoches in trees, midrash in the under-brush, footnotes to sermons in the stones, and trope in every-thing." How charming, and how falsifyingly literal! But the anti-quary and the rhetorician, though they may quarrel in public, embrace sweatily and breathlessly in closets; and to follow such advice, however at once fresh and venerable it may seem, is once again to confirm all the fuss and bother, to help augment with real figures the empty ledgers of the rhetorician, he "who seemèd busyer than he was."

No, no: confound him and his kind. Take his precious and widely used utensil—for example, the distinction between meta-phor and synecdoche. It is a distinction that contrives to lump together on one side parts for wholes, wholes for parts, labels for containers, handles for chests, cousins for siblings, opposites for opposites, and a multitude of others. In the light—or rather the darkness—of it, if, enraged, I fling my dinner napkin at the rhetorician instead of the cast-iron pot, I do so in metaphor; but if the matching cloth pot-holder, then in metonymy. Take this distinction, then, with you on your walk. Go up into the low hills, and find the first point of prospect you come to from which to regard the road along—and up—which you have come, and the higher hills far around and beyond. Look across at the hills: consider the graying and bluing that goes on in the watercolor of what you see, the array of tints that makes for layer on layer of distant height. Then look down along the path you have taken: observe the three tiny walkers, at various removes behind and below where you are now, one moving like a bug as seen from above, the others strokes of moving color at a level distance.

Now is the time to take out your utensil to cut up the appear-ances into portions of truth. Is the bluing of the hills then a metaphor for distance? Or a metonymy? What of the conven-tions of perspective that shrink your following travelers to minus-cules or even dots? They alter by trope, but which one? And the ultimate question that emerges from these, the question that reigns over all such subjects: does the two-dimensional world of drawing make its representations of three-dimensional space by metonymy, the two for the three? Or by metaphor? The world of the plane cannot imagine, even on the analogy of its own perception of the relations of point, line, and polygon within it, the for us inevitable step into solid space. For the plane, that would be the wildest metaphorical leap. Which, then?

Carry the question home with you from your walk. The question itself—preserved from the rotting of easy answer by your botanizing care—will be more fruitful than a dozen dry verses or a dozen dry deconstructions. Keep such questions: the poet will taste of their sweetness, long after they have dried. The rhetorician will experience their bitterness, and his own acute indigestion.

We Can Reclaim Truth from the Lies of Writing   The scribbler of verses will have it, for instance, that "Morning is a shopping list." By this he or she will mean to employ a once pointed and poignant device—that of the widow lamenting in springtime who says "Sorrow is my own yard," now rotted into the foul cuteness of "Happiness is a cuddly kitten," or the like. For such a scribbler the morning will indeed shrink to something short, fragile, injunctive, and reproachful, in a grossly literal kind of contraction. But when one is free of the foolishness of writing, one can awaken and seize the morning, take it in hand like a shopping list, and read it as a prophecy whose continuation is its own fulfillment. This is a list whereon necessities and superflux, designs and impulses, are all present; a list whereon the very orders of priority, or of implicit route through the day's avenues, themselves embody yet another order of choice and chance. Some lists contain works and plays all mingled higgledy-piggledy, that messiness being the greatest of self-indulgences in itself; some will start or end with what one buys laughing, some with the shops one visits in pain and tears. The lists will thus represent the rarities and repetitions of each new day, each old morning—one of the new, more of the old. And the "is" of the bad writer's little nastiness will be turned toward the noble work of trope: shuttling back and forth between identity and predication, touching neither, but humming away in the energy of its doings, the "is" will truly couple. And the list itself will have been written—even the dreadful reminder of one, black item—by you and necessity together, setting out, even if not to end the day, hand in hand.

I

Short Fictions and Fables

In the Year of the Comet

On an important, mild March night of that year, it was the very best boy, the quietest and most solemn, the Wise Son who rose from his place, crossed the bright, hushed room, and, shutting the door that was to have been left open, suddenly started to ask the Wrong Question. It was the same selfish and outrageous query that the Wicked Son, the ruffian, closeted that night with his family almost—but not quite—against his will, had never failed to ask before. As if once a year he might redeem himself by playing the unfailing straight man! And as the wise brother asked his question, betrayed his new nature, he barely smiled. It was as if, perhaps, it had been he himself who had crept through the house late that afternoon, moving through long shadows, silently as the motes moved in the vanishing sunlight, putting little scraps of Something Forbidden in all the dish cupboards, disordering the traditional order of the courses of the meal soon to be served.

And the Wicked Son! Which of these changelings seemed more horrible? He slouched in from the street corner, clad in the black that startled always by seeming somehow, sickeningly, no sober color, tonight, as always, never without a knife, and suddenly started dissolving into someone else. A vague recollection from a mirror in childhood, perhaps, or an image from some old photograph he preferred never to remember. But in any case, a presence against which his usual smirk, his studied and dreadful gestures (the combing of black hair back, comb and left hand alternately caressing; the continually averted glance that assaulted rather than retreated) seemed always aimed. He glanced slowly and questioningly about the shining room, rich in silver and pearly linen and burgundy

From *Noble Savage* 2 (1961): 161–64.

velvet-tasseled cushions, as if the whole scene were new to him, and as if the not-yet-astonished faces of relatives about him were those of a precious set of dependents, just then given over to his care. No one present cared to think of what he would do next. Only his mother remembered that he was one of the sons after all, and not, by reason of the knife *(my God, the knife!)* one of the Others.

The Wicked Son began to weep.

All this was surely bad enough. There was no reclining on the winy cushions then, but all sitting bolt upright like candles and the breaths of all bated with wonder and unsteady as threatened flames. But then hysteria seized the mother and she began to mutter and sob to herself (not hearing the Simple Son, the dummer, hulking over his plate and minimally filled wineglass across the table from her, begin to address the gnarled, deaf great-uncle placed next to him in accents at once conversational, intense, and amused: *"If nature be opposed to miracles, not only the distinction betwixt vice and virtue is natural, but also every event, which has ever happen'd in the world . . ."* and he paused to rub his hair and chin and murmur into his plate for a moment before continuing: *"In saying then, that the sentiments of vice and virtue are natural in this sense, we make no very extraordinary discovery . . ."*). But the mother heard none of this, so intent was she on the very beginning of abandoning herself to violences of the mind, so clearly did there ring again and again in her ears the miraculous utterance of the fourth boy, the one who sat always by her and who had to be attended to and wiped and stroked continually, the one who said only "Va, va, veh" in no language, the one who brought with him into the world some natural rebuke for pride taken in sons. He had turned to her, the sudden unnatural brightness in his idiot eye taken from no flush of wine or flash of candlestick, glanced at his brother, the weeping thug, and apropos everything (for the only time in his life, apropos anything) began to ask the Right First Question.

Who was to answer? Portions of text in a dead vernacular provided no response. Commentaries in the continuing hieratic dialect seemed mean and parochial. Wiseguy, the Bright Boy gone wrong, looked up with a sneer only. And the Father, he who should guide the wise, put down the wicked, instruct the simple, and honor the idiotic with the tokens of discourse, what does he say? He hunches up in his purple pillows, giggling softly. And the others? They stare and stare, transfixed in silences of their own, until suddenly, for each, reality flies up like an escaping windowshade revealing the present world behind, flaring with immediacy, stripped bare of the clouds of sense.

Outside, the comet shone at its brightest for the year, spread streaming across the peculiar graying sky (as if the rich black of frosty nights had had milk poured in it), huge head and forked, trailing beard, resembling now more than ever an inept engraving, bright not only with its own dusty light, but increased with the diffuse possibility of prophecy, perhaps, for those few watchers who had left their houses to gather in the middle of well-paved suburban streets, or to climb little hillocks near the post-office building to see more clearly.

For those who remained within, in worlds transformed by real signs and unnatural wonders, there was only the moment to contemplate before the uneasy order of the usual was restored, before virtues and ailments rejoined their identities: before the Best Boy became earnest and nervous again, before the Cool One shrugged off his skullcap, made love to his hair, and rejoined vile companions, before fools became fools and fathers, Fathers again. Roles in old ceremonies were properly filled. (The comet, meanwhile, had passed its perihelion, and, like any conceivable instant of time, had started to veer away on its path of no return, its devoted band of observers, all unaware of this imperceptible and irrevocable event, continuing either to stand about in groups or to head for their own homes, the night sky remaining unchanged from accustomed pallor.) Everyone sitting at the long, white table, expanded with boards and covered with felt pads and the richest damask, everyone beginning to look at each other's faces again in order to discover who he himself was, everyone beginning to think of his turn to participate, to read, to pour, to clear or serve, to pass, to interrupt, to question, to sing, to agree, to frolic, to comment, to restrain, to belch, to be—everyone, in fact, who planned in any way to go on with it all after what had nevertheless most undeniably occurred, adjusted himself in his seat, sat or lay back, and began the very difficult process of getting to know that, of course, it had all not been here. That it had been in the neighbors' house where it had happened.

Tales of the Supernatural

The Mummy's Hand

This story has happened so many times that to add one more account to the store would not appreciably add weight to the load of attested witness. But after what we have just been hearing—about that strange bean that appeared to be made of dust, and about the outcry from the cup of broth—I cannot refrain from sharing with you the sense of the inexpressible that overcame me, let alone the almost strangling horror, on that ordinary November evening, warmed by the lights in shop windows and the bustle of homecoming in the city streets.

The child returning from an after-school visit with a friend had just rounded the corner of the block on which she lived, and was heading uphill, past a druggist's window in which various herbs and roots lay disposed in apothecary's jars, in among the cosmetics. One gnarled, grayish root might have suggested to her the withered or petrified hand of some ancient mummy if, indeed, she had ever seen even a picture of such an object. But she had not. The word *mummy* lay in a pool of shadowy imprecision for her. She knew of ancient Egyptian burial practices from books, and had indeed seen illustrations of sarcophagi; but what she had always imagined the embalmed corpse within to resemble was inextricable from her usual term of maternal endearment. She thought of—she felt, rather—a mother, eternally preserved, breasts flattened and bound but emblematic, in low relief, of an unending nurture. Not in milk, nor in a later warmth—this nurture gave of a continuing idolization of origin, of the place where one had once been, but dare not go again, a place guarded by the very mummification of

From *Canto* 4, no. 11 (1981).

disembodied presence into something like a nasty, shriveled statue, a meeting-place of bone and stone. She imagined the mummy, sitting up rather than lying down, something cross-legged, and pre-Columbian looking.

She was not prepared, then, for the events that soon occurred. Nor, indeed, was I, although perhaps overripe, as we all are, for a canard or hoax, damaged rather than liberated by our skepticism—lulled by it, even. As we met that evening in the elevator of the apartment house then, and greeted each other with the nods of Manhattan neighbors, the question as to which of us was more truly innocent, and which more armored— perhaps even more chained—by experience, lay just out of reach, away from apparent applicability, like the series of floors behind the numbered doors that flew downward through the lozenges formed by the metal gate. It was only after the elevator had stopped at her floor, after the door had opened, that anything was overtly manifested. But then her father appeared from their apartment, whose door was out of sight from the elevator, and confronted us with a dark look on his face. A large, rectangular, velvet-covered box was held out before him in both hands as he stooped slightly in the light of the dim hallway. And then she half-turned to me with a rather upsetting version playing across her mouth of the smile on Leonardo's John the Baptist, pointing likewise across her body at the figure standing before us outside the elevator.

Years and years later, in another kind of life, that moment would return to me in a different form. Far away from there, in a house above a lake, for example: sitting in the July evening with a companion, playing, four-hands, *Our Friendship Is Unchanging*, it was natural that I should wonder, when the room darkened so that we had to turn on the lamp with its fringed shade above the music rack, what the changing light implied for the meaning of what we were doing. But more uncanny was the sense of transition, of a threshold crossed, when we had ourselves to intercross hands, her left now playing below my right, problematically distracting us from the business at hand, which was, of course, our own imaginative commerce with the parallel sixths we were producing. It was then that the extra set of fingers seemed to emerge, not from the darkness behind or below us, but from the music itself. It was there when a page needed turning—as if by a gust of appreciative breeze—or to rub gently across a momentarily perplexed brow, and, at the end of the evening, to slam the lid down on the keyboard, sadly but loudly, in long, slow vengefulness rather than rage. But requiring vengeance for what, I never knew, nor did my companion: for errors of memory? for misreadings of what is ambiguous in the most commonplace darknesses? for words mistaken and for self-betrayals? Perhaps it was the very despair of the event itself, despair of ever appropriately representing in altered form the moment in the elevator years before mingled with the heartbreaking knowledge that it could not return to it unchanged. This is surely the most reasonable explanation; on bad, sleepless nights I have often been grateful for its plausibility.

The Driveway

On an August evening, on a quiet street whose lamps bent down from their posts as if under the homely burden of darkened leaves, he found himself, having driven somewhat more than halfway down the block, turning into a driveway. It led to an unlit house he had never known of, let alone seen, or considered, or entered. But it was a driveway he would get to know so intimately that even "know well" would seem an irrelevant description of his grasp of it, or its of him.

Had he run out of gas—or stopped to change a tire, or to ask for a glass of water or for directions—and there encountered a person, soft as the shadows in which she sat waiting, marked by the single disfigurement he had always craved and feared to crave, this would have been a different story. The touches of moonlight that contested the older darkness for possession of her lap, her hair, would themselves have seemed to interpret this encounter for him. The room, its daybed, its pictures hung in darkness and whose glass occasionally flashed an image of light not their own; the house, with its unknown other rooms awaiting eventual exploration; the garden, with its plots and hedges; and, yes, the driveway itself—these would have become part of his life. Or, if you prefer, a new life, starting from some point between the time he braked and turned the car's wheel left and the encounter in the room, might have grown out of all these, as well as in and among them.

But as it was, the chattering whispers of the gravel, as he moved slowly along toward whatever was to be, grew louder and deeper and more overwhelmingly like the sound of a voice that he had often heard, low and rasping inside his head, rebuking him for something ever unspecified, in childhood. Beyond this, it could not be told whether he knew what was happening to him. Did he feel, in the last minutes, that some warlock of bad punning had, literally, turned him into the driveway? Some halfwit son of the great metamorphoser, Circe? Or did he feel that something of his old life would, with some justice, remain eternally embodied—giving meaning to, even as it lay imprisoned—in a driveway, an emblem of approach? Or was it simply that he knew nothing of what was happening then and there as language itself—whether playful, in the moonlit summer night, or heavily sad and with a sense of wearying necessity, in the shadow of still unspeaking leaves—laughed, coughed, shivered, or turned, and brought it all about? In any event, before he could reach the house he had become the driveway, and there was no doubt about what that could "mean" any more.

The Thing on the Beach

"At the end, all the world was America," wrote John Keye somewhere in his journals, but for us, at the end of that late summer afternoon, all was still sand and air and ocean, framed by the darkness of pines beyond that kept their distance from the scene and yet at the same time inhered in the pine-green troughs of the water. The wind sang a sea-song of alternations, up and down, hard then low, loud then soft; it was neither the weather nor the time of day for fishing. We sat, content to muse on the relation of the sea of figure to the literal shore—from which, it need hardly be said, we were doing the musing—and waiting for the chill and the long shadows to reach out from the dunes and bring us back.

For we were not only on the shifting margin of the sea but on the fringes of the woods as well, as if thereby to show how we were, generally, dwelling on the selvage of our lives, how at this point we were just out of the woods but not away from them. Something far beyond any wind we could feel sent up across the water the brushwork of light, going up and down among the rollers. We could see that, were we out there past the rolling breakers, all that could be seen of us from the beach would be our heads, bobbing up and down like jetsam that might be scarcely worth the salvage. We were at our wits' end, you see, all that summer, knowing so well how our line was playing out and that we might be only fancying the reassuring tugs we felt from whatever we had, so to speak, hooked. We had probably hooked nothing, and in this case might lose our line nonetheless, and to lose that line was to lose oneself. We all knew this, and we saw ourselves as lost in any case. Alf and Ralph were there, and Max and Didi and Deve, and we had not yet wearied of one another, so that it might not have mattered which of us, looking away from our little group, up along the beach, saw the thing first.

But in fact it did matter, because, you see, I was the one; it matters now to me because I have never been the same since that afternoon. I call what I saw a "thing" because it was in any event not a person, exactly, nor a place. It was more like something happening to a person, in a place—just, indeed, as my awareness of it, my sense of what I was seeing, was something happening *to* a place (that part of the beach, in fact), *in* a person, namely myself. But more of this in a moment. The fact was that I saw, against the background of shimmering haze into which the broad beach vanished a half-mile or so northeast along it, a distant group about the size of our own and, nearest us, one of their number who was looking over toward me. The Thing itself had taken shape midway between us, rising slowly up from the indeterminacy of shadow in the sand; it stood, facing in our direction, its parted legs allowing me to see, between them, the other, more distant person and his companions. It was not a shadow, nor yet a mirage; could I have approached it, I might have perceived a sort of seam, like the one that bisects the surface of figures cast in certain molds, dividing its two sides—the half that I saw, and the other half, which I knew somehow was not a back. The dark side of the phenomenon would have resembled some distorted version of myself, as seen through squinted eyes at twice the distance. The side of the thing I could see indeed resembled a view of the distant person:

blue trunks, dark hair on a sunburned body. But there was a quality of painted generalization about the figure-thing itself, as if a telescope trained on it could resolve clearly only the limited visual information—outline, color, inferential shape of arm and leg, rough facial contour—that distance could yield up to the unaided eye. Its face was like a rumor of a familiar truth.

Were the thing a person, it would have been monstrous. Were it a representation—a dummy of some kind—it would have been witty and comical. But it was made of other stuff. It was the effigy of an event, certainly more *like* a person than like styrofoam or papier-mâché or whatever, but certainly of a very different sort of substantiality. However its parts were joined—it was surely the work of the man way down the beach as well as my own—they fitted perfectly. His perception of me was clapped together with mine of him, like the Magdeburg hemispheres that were joined by the vacuum they surrounded. They must have met, these two elements, somewhere midway between us, because of some prank of reflection. The other side of the thing was in brown trunks, somewhat the color of mine, but corrected for shadow and distance, standing with legs apart and looking down toward my counterpart.

Then the beach darkened. I looked up and out at the towering clouds that had blown across the sun for a moment. When I looked back, the thing had gone. Nor did it return. What terrified me so was that it was on the beach itself that it appeared, not out at sea, where I felt it more properly belonged. It seemed to have been out of its habitat, and I hope that it was back into the water that it vanished. I never told the others about all this. But as I said, I have never been the same, as if I had stepped into a pool of shadow—like one sharply outlined on the hot concrete of a walk—and been unable thereafter to withdraw my foot from the consequences of the step. It was just as well that Alf and Ralph, that Max and Deve and Didi did not have to cope with any of this.

The Speaking Pictures

All this is happening to us this afternoon, I think, because silence has lost its comforting music for us, and its wisdom. We have been walking quietly together among the dustiest galleries of the Museum. Our own reticence about discourse, and the hush of these large, empty chambers, unvisited save by ourselves, have become mixed with the gray, indeterminate illumination from the skylights. The effect has been to lose, for the silence, the specificity it had when we first entered the Museum together, an hour ago, from the noisy streets.

In any event, we seem to have wandered away from everyone else, into some sort of reserve collection. Totally unfamiliar paintings, by artists even you have never heard of, have been hung here, rather haphazardly. From the far, darkened end of the large room we are now in, there seem to be sounds of distant voices, low voices strangely amplified, else they should not be audible from rooms away. We approach this shadowy region of sound, walking slowly together, mindful of what we feel for each other, and for each other's sorrow.

ॐ

What we have first is a lamplit interior, mostly in shadow; a young man holds aside a curtain into an alcove that we cannot see into but that he has just been regarding. His finger on his lips, looking out at us with a glance half of plea and half of reproach, he nonetheless breaks his own silence, as his voice comes to us from one of the dark corners of the room behind him.

"Here is the Penelope of Memory, undoing her work in the evening lamplight. At midnight now she has forgotten even her own name, and only the morning sun, falling across her half-empty bed, weaves its way into her hair and awakens the figure of her name, her nature and her task; so that, imitating herself, she can set to work in her own image again each day."

ॐ

It is easy to overlook the cabinet-painting in the corner; its small size, the way in which it is shadowed by its placement and by the afternoon light, would make us tend to pass it by, were it not for a loud whispering that draws us over to its corner. It can now be seen to represent a middle-aged man, strong and, in all likelihood, possessed of some kind of wisdom, standing by a stream in a clearing in the woods. Upstream from him, absorbed in something he holds in his hand, is a youth. (The title of the picture, *The Stream*, is either coyly enigmatic, if the artist's own, or else irrelevant, if carelessly chosen by a curator.) A large rock in the foreground, partly in the stream and partly out of it, turns out to be the source of the whispers, which do not in fact come from the stream itself. The rock's message is brief:

"The young man hides from the thought of Death by not mentioning its name, the older man, by constant allusion to it."

&

As we turn a corner and walk down a long gallery, full of dusty plaster casts of classical figures, a low voice speaks to us from a darkened alcove, through a low entrance off the gallery; it is a low, humane contralto, loving and sensible in its inflections, tinted faintly with some kind of Germanic accent. As we pass, it is saying:

"We have two compulsions that, far from competing with each other, defer in mutual respect and appear to leave one another's territory unmolested. One is the desire to innovate. The other is to achieve repetition. Most of us never discover that they are indeed in collusion, with the sad consequences for us that when we strive to originate, we only succeed in repeating the past; and when, conversely, we attempt to recapitulate what was once done, we can only produce a dreadful travesty, one that looks to have been the result of a strained but novel wit. It is only unwittingly that we perform the repetitions, and without consciously desiring or contriving to do so that we can originate. Most of us never learn the difference between old and new in any case. Those who do learn to laugh and cry at it."

Those of us who feel the need to do so go into the alcove to inspect the picture that has spoken. It almost goes without saying that it is an American sunrise, on an eastern shore, the scene divided equally between sea and sky.

&

Finally, just before leaving, we approach a square canvas. 100 × 100 cm, centered on a flat, white ground, an open circle, diameter 60 cm, its circumference an ultramarine line 2 mm wide. Concentric, within, a smaller circle, diameter 20 cm, its soft-penciled circumference 1 mm in width. In this instance, the whole painting appears to speak to us, in a gentle but somewhat impatient tone. Despite our temptation to hear—to want to hear—the voice as coming from the middle of the smaller circle, we had indeed to confess that its source could not be so located. What it had to say seemed, in view of its abstract and nearly minimal quality (nearly: even a grain of sand and its shadow are nearly, but not quite, elemental), to be inappropriately long, unless it were taken as a kind of afterword to what the other pictures had spoken.

"I know what you are asking me: Am I not a representation of the very problem of picturing what I represent? A physical metaphor, too blue, too objectlike, to be any more than a picture of my circle; yet that gross blue periphery itself dreams of a gentler touch, a frailer penciled way of getting at the immaterial form, as if at any moment the inner dream of what a circle truly is could be erased in a kind of waking. Oh yes, circles are a problem: diagrams always say less than portraits, but for a circle, any diagram, any schematic, notational, minimal picture is already too much. The thinnest of ruled lines is no stick figure of the Euclidean entity, but might as well be the fleshiest of Rubensian bodies, part of the world yielded up by the most loaded of brushes. Any drawn circle is an overdoing of the matter of idea.

So that what I am *of* is a more profound but elusive matter than what I apparently am, and I would suggest that you not pursue that, but rather listen to what I have to say. *That*—what I say now—is the image I create, and indeed project. For the painted or drawn Image lies somewhere in space between the Picture and the Depicted; but it can and must be translated to a point somewhere between the Picture and the Observer, even as it hangs between us at this very moment, breathing in an atmosphere of my voice. The Image is like a likeness—like, indeed, similarity itself—in that it mediates, and in that it must be invented. (As when the child, bringing us a handful of weeds and leaves, says "Show me a game of grass," so that we teach him the degrees of green and the rudiments of form, then creates for himself the reality not only of blades and leaves, or even of greens, but of what likeness and unlikeness are as well.)

Pictures that, unlike myself, deny that they are of anything, tell lies against what they depict and, however unwittingly, defend themselves thus against the world of too many pictures, of too many modes of picturing. Such pictures have come along too late to take joy in their relation to, say, a chair that might have sat for them, a chair in a studio they both depicted as well and were conceived and born in. Too late for that—and too early to rejoice in the crowds of painted chairs that, by being seen properly askew and thereby depicted, might produce Images of the true chair—all these late pictures lie, in addition, against where their Images are located. But I know that region. And now you do.

The Tales

"In other words," he continued, taking what had just been said in a new sense, "in other words—" But one's memory of exactly how he continued—of what in fact the other words precisely were—could so easily fade into the more powerful and absorbing memory of where we all were at the time, disposed in a grouping at once fond, casual, and playful enough to be possibly serious.

It was the kind of group that might have assembled in any season, for any appropriate purpose. In winter, for example, on a night of blizzard: trains delayed for hours, roads best left alone, each of the group forced to stay in, or down-, town, collecting at their club. In this case, each of them believed himself to be one of the club ghosts for whom the more active and promiscuously genial members were bores, but who loved the generous spaces and textures of the building's noble rooms. They were all acquainted, but far from friends, and yet that evening they had discovered, at dinner, their community of isolation from the more eminently clubbable other members. They sat before the massive fireplace, under the magnificent view of Petra by Frederick Church, its rock and sunset reds reflected in the active light from the burning logs. Dinner over, they drank, and talked, and one might have broken in on their discourse at just such a point as this moment of paraphrase.

Or it might just as well have collected, this circle of casual friends, on a clear summer night, far below Cygnus and Lyra together overhead, on the afterdeck of an ocean liner. Young men and women who eschewed the idiocies of Bingo and funny-hat events, who perhaps had danced some, or walked briskly about in the dark air, now gathered near the stern. In the lee of stacked deck-chairs, they sat or stood about. In the darkness—but also in the light of the immense distances above, all about, and even below—in this informed and annotated darkness, whatever intimacies preexisted this evening, intimacies between couples or pairs of companions, dissolved into the momentary community.

Or else the water lapped at the stone fortifications around the tiny historic harbor, the statue of Freedom at the entrance barely visible, early on an April night, against the water of the gulf behind it. A group sat at three or four adjoining tables at the tavern, a group that had collected itself at a beautiful but not-often-frequented ancient site a day or so before. There was no actual moment of contract that pierced the translucent shell of common interest, mutual approval, and even a gleam of satisfaction on the part of each at being able to find and acquire such a pleasant group among whom he or she would be delighted to be discerned. They merely found themselves traveling together without contrivance, and at most by some surprise of design. Their slight but edifying knowledge of the language, their sense of history, their shared self-respect—all of these allowed their late and delicate repast to become a kind of symposium. In it, the interruption, the interjected overture to the paraphrase that would profitably follow, seemed itself like the gravest of courtesies in some charming and meticulously revived country dance.

But in fact, it was a night in late October, and we had been at the mountain-lodge all day—with a hundred or more others who had all left by then—for the funeral of our common friend, who was buried that afternoon at sundown in one of his own nearby meadows. We were waiting for a chartered bus that had been delayed by several hours, and had taken warmth, food, and drink at the resort inn; we were a random subgroup of a loosely connected larger one, and the ad hoc intimacy of the circumstances played with and against the web of our interconnections, through the missing center of our departed common friend, blowing about it like a breeze. None of us had known one another more than casually. The visual scene itself had been spectacular, in the manner of darkening mountains, with enough of the sublime imprinted upon it by the occasion so as to affect the black night sky outside the room where we waited and talked. We had, in fact, to take the natural darkness as some kind of radiance.

No ceremony of any preordained sort added its shadow to those that already embraced us. And yet all evening, whatever little procedural rules we had developed, within the ground rules of the day's formal rituals, seemed always to have been there. They were like furniture that normally recedes into the interior design of a room but that jumps out at you, so to speak, when suddenly needed, for a table-surface, say, or a seat. So it was with the casual but assured ways in which we framed, and gestured about, what was being said. All the more reason, then, that the *sense* of the exact words of his paraphrase of the preceding remarks, the words that have been perhaps significantly forgotten, should be as easy to remember as the words themselves were not.

So that "In other words, we're going to tell stories now, as in some old story?" seemed to connect, to couple the whole earlier part of the evening with what was to follow. It was a coupling that partook of neither phase in essence or form—nothing had been said before, you understand, about what *would* be done. Yet it was anchored firmly and deeply in the substance of what preceded and followed it, without thereby enforcing a visible division, a seam or scar or line of weld, along the surface of what was happening.

There was no need for anyone to say "I'm sure that each of us has experienced something that would ordinarily . . . ," for whatever that could mean to what we were all to say in the next few hours was understood. It seemed to inhere in the scene, the grouping, the moment of the year and our lives. The first story was told in response to the original "In other words . . ." but seemed, as I remember, to flow utterly smoothly, liquidly from that response which may have begun "Well, I . . ." In any event, the tales began to be told; and during the course of the night— the bus did not arrive until 2:00 A.M.—most of us told several, often reminded, by hearing one of the others, of one that he or she had originally intended to tell.

The astonishing thing was that everybody seemed, a few weeks afterward, to have remembered the occasion differently. Not the scene, the ambiance, the tone, the feeling the group had about itself. In fact, everything that I have set down with any certainty could have been done so by any of us—even the initiating "In other words . . ." was something nobody forgot. But you would think that the heart of the matter lay in the stories themselves, and there remained a great difference of opinion about those. The few low conversations that continued on the bus that night before almost everyone slept were, as far as I know, all confined to other matters. It was not until two weeks later, when I happened to encounter Hagedorn, who had been there, at another sort of gathering entirely, that the astonishing matter of the stories came to light.

I was reaching for a drink across a crowded bar-table—it was, I recall, an Old Fashioned, generously embittered—in an apartment high above Manhattan, brushing past another man who was turning away, a newly acquired drink in hand, when I recognized him. We retired to a windowed corner and gazed out at the November sky flooding its gray darkness over Central Park below. I reminded him of a story I remembered him having told after the funeral on the mountain; to our common astonishment, he denied having told it. I then recalled other tales, other tellers; so did he. Both of us agreed that we had remembered the stories clearly, but could associate them with their tellers in only a few cases. Neither of us remembered the same stories, and even as we stood there, summoning up stories and voices from imaginary places around the dark lounge of the inn where our memories had stored them, we were in total disagreement.

Our amazement at this, and our subsequent researches during the next week—resurrecting the list of those present, getting addresses and so forth, framing a letter explaining our puzzlement and asking for assistance—produced a confirmation that a mystery existed. Everyone we could reach recollected a different group of stories, associated with idiosyncratic attributions of authorship. Proposed explanations ranged from weakness of memory, to a mutual but unconspired-in perversity that had swept us all afterward, causing us all tacitly to agree to disagree; there was even the poignant but implausible suggestion that the stories had all come from one narrator, and that all of us, dozing off intermittently in the mountain air, both reassigned the tales to different members of the group and dreamily incorporated one or two ourselves, as having been of our own telling. In this case, each person's period of slumber would have accounted for the material later unfamiliar. Some of us had even forgotten which, of the several tales we might have told, we actually did.

Hagedorn and I eventually asked each of the group to send all the others a written version of the one tale he or she remembered most clearly. This was some way, I supposed, of reconstituting the event of the storytelling so that it would become the same kind of common property as most remembered social occasions—a hard, central structure of verifiable fact radiating, in the room of memory, a warmth of private, indeed secret, heat, heat that no verifying account could acknowledge to exist, let alone try to describe. In our own case, there was no metal or brick or ceramic, the stove, as it were, having dissolved into the radiant heat; what we wanted was at least a model or drawing of the stove of substance. What we finally acquired, each of us, was a group of texts only one of which each could remember—if only remember, in at least one case, having written in response to the letter we sent around—but all of which were made to fit into a room, a space, of intense remembrance.

And they are more than enough. Like a stove in a small, cold room in which a thinker sits writing, they emanate question after warming question: Is a written text more durable than a memory or not? Does whichever lasts longer pay for this resistance to ruin in bits of authenticity? Suppose that the stories we all received in the mail were made up at the last moment, that, in fact, nobody sent a tale actually remembered? What then? What about the nature of the tales themselves: *could* they have been told that night?

These questions, and questions about them, continue to be exhaled by the stories. I rarely see any of the other people very much, and when I do there is little mention of the whole matter, but no want—I have never felt any want—of silent, deep acknowledgment. It is as if the little collection of xeroxed leaves, now beginning to turn brown at the edges, had become itself, for each owner of it, a unique exemplar. Some of them have, I gather, been bound handsomely in leather or plainly in buckram; some repose in spring-binders or manila folders. Mine, at least, remains unannotated. But all embody a kind of purity in their own association, as members of a textual group: however interpreted by each of us, nonetheless unchangeable.

The Beginning

"Bang!" (That is how so many ambitious narratives would like to start out; but they always avoid this particular tetragrammaton, this four-lettered unutterable, as if thereby to ward off ill-luck. The specific "Bang" with which I commence may echo, for all I know, with the German word of fear—meaning "alarmed" or "frightened"—fear in this case of true explosion. Not a catastrophic event in a story, but the kind of origin that begins with recoil and withdrawal, only to erupt into light and sound. Or fear, perhaps, of the loss of silence, or fear of some possible chain reaction that might overtake and consume the whole narrative tail that was to have been wagged by the beginning. That was certainly not my intention; and while I must feel myself to be something unattempted yet in prose, I have no wish to be undecipherable—although, as we tend to forget, every unreadable message is unreadable in its own way, uniquely, while all significant utterances partake of the ordinariness of those like, "Here's your change" and "There's the airport." Nor is "Bang" the name of the Danish doctor who identified the bacillus that causes cows to abort their calves—although I could easily have commenced by calling out that name, awakening not himself but, say, his great-grandson, now an undergraduate at a British university. Why awaken him? Because he might groan sleepily in response, crawl out of bed, shivering, and throw open the heavy stuff curtaining his window. He would stare out at the mitigated picturesqueness of Tudor brickwork pelted with raw February rain, and remember, after all, what day it was. And, full of the unique *kind* of special quality the morning had for him—and would have, for others who could not know at that moment that they were to share with him the consequences of the day's uniqueness—he would return to his bed and reach under it. He would retrieve from his left shoe the small, rather frightening object, small enough to absorb all of the concentrated and continuing attention of obsession with it. And he would start moving into, and thereby creating, the world of events contingent upon events, of *post* and *propter,* which are one's bones and sinews. But it is not to awaken young Bang that I start out as I do—he may very well have his day, in any case. The "B" of beginnings is, appropriately, the alphabet's second letter; it is almost as if, in initiations, we were burying the top card before dealing ourselves the hand, or swallowing the aspiring "A" in order to feed the first subsequent breath. Otherwise I might begin with "Ahem!"—or with the more archaic, attention-getting *"Hwaet"* or "There was this guy who . . ." or the contemporary, loose-jointed "Like, I mean, you know": the doormen of our houses. But I start out with a moderately big bang of origination, for it is only fables that are able to compose themselves, to deny their derivations. A relative of mine tells of a visionary builder of thinking machines— "artificial intelligence" is, I believe, what he called his field of work—who, when asked how he would know that he had successfully simulated human consciousness, replied "When I've built something that refuses to—that *can't*—acknowledge that I designed and built it." But what he would have simulated in such a case would be not a person—people acknowledge parents, Creators, their own earlier lives, at an alarming rate—but a fable, a fiction. In fables, the "A" of authorship, of authority, or authenticity, is no long prior to the "B" of beginnings, but subsequent to it. Somewhere along the line, for example, I will have invented the author of my wanderings, one "John Hollander," say, perhaps in some dream that might be described later on. But no matter. This beginning is over, and if with so much violence, so much dispersal of energy that all the usual following sequence of events was consumed in the heat and light of that opening bang, then at least a beginning that has led, although elliptically, to an inevitable sort of conclusion:) ". . . *and that is all that is known of the matter to this day.* "

The Treasure Hunt

The hunt was on. Murmurings of interpretation, cries of *trouvaille*, the sounds of laughter and delight, all echoed under the large, high porte cochere at the side of the house, from which the treasure hunt started out. The players came from some distance around the local corner of the county; the course appeared to be wide-ranging, intricate, challenging, and generous; the weather was fine, and nothing promised to darken the afternoon. The players, in particular: how could these young people running through the light woods in their summer clothes be anything but figures of light, checkered only with lovely, moving shade? —Even figures of light that would itself darken into misfortune, disease, sorrow, and the descending pall of unwitting cruelty that would come upon them with age? One's view of them would of course depend upon what one thought the relation of light to shadow is all about. But as they snapped twigs underfoot, or padded over the stretches of pine needles that lay along the obvious course suggested by the first bright clue, these youths, players of a ridiculous summer game, beauties or sillies or both as they variously were, became for a while people of the book. Laughter and motion, one might object, and the light breathing of hope: why weigh it down with all that?

Because each clue they came upon was not so much a puzzle to be solved as a bit of scripture to be understood and applied to life, an allegory to be loved not only for what it yielded up, but for the very knots and twists in its texture that would eventually be doing the yielding, and that would give of themselves, rather than of something they merely enwrapped. And each interpretation of the written words of a clue yielded nothing trivial—a Fact, a Truth, a Way—but instead pointed out something to-

From *Conjunctions* 2 (1985). Written in 1982.

ward which a way had to be found. And that way would lead to a new text.

Let me explain.

> Blest be the ties that bind;
> Seek, then, and ye shall find.

on the third clue led two of the searchers to the railroad tracks under which one had to walk on the way to the lake, and then to a wardrobe in the master bedroom, erring, both times, in their ingenuity. But two of the younger ones, Star and Aviva, considered the clue in a different way: they sang the first line of the couplet in its old, hymnal setting—*sol, sol-re, sol, fa-re, fami*—and then Star recalled his uncle who used to sing, to the same tune, *"I'd rather have fingers than toes"* while Aviva concluded that any limerick would fit the tune as well. They rejoiced momentarily in their fingers, touched themselves and each other lightly, and considered the second line of the clue. It came from Matthew 7:7, and the gospel aside, "their" Matthew was the gardener, who was full of wildly improbably local folklore, and always good for the whereabouts of a previously undiscovered raspberry bush. They wandered from the gatehouse, where the third clue had been affixed, to the rose garden, where Matthew could not be found, then on into the house to inquire of one of the grownups where Matthew might be. Rushing past the piano in the front parlor, Aviva dislodged a pile of books on the swivel-stool and, behold, inserted in the obvious place in an old hymnal was the fourth clue. A happy accident, yes, but one that could not have happened without all the mistakes about the third clue.

It was not, then, a mere matter of problem solving. We have heard of how, in order to hit the mark, we must aim at it, of course, but simultaneously think of aiming somewhere else—to one side, beyond it, or whatever—in order to align eye and spirit. We know fables of finding one's way in the woods, or of getting some kind of distance from one's own searching, lest the lost object stare us in the face without being seen itself. But such was not the case with these clues and their consequences for the treasure hunt. Interpreting them involved bringing life—active, random, pointless, silly, and profound—to bear on the artlessly contrived and transparently obscure texts. It required the phases and episodes that surrounded the reading of the clues to become parables themselves.

The Treasure itself—there is a problem here: the term *treasure* confuses several matters—the treasure that had been promised, the treasure actually sought by each of the young people, the treasure actually attained by the winners, and the consolation prizes that the losers would contrive to award to themselves, from the gathered gold of the late afternoon sunlight and from the assembled fragments of the particular course each had taken. These were, and are, all quite different. The treasure of the hunt itself was the guerdon of completing it, was running about so that, somehow, the treasure would be found by somebody or other. The actual hidden treasure—the promised one—was in fact in the attic of the great, old, dusty dolls' house in the attic chamber that used to be the children's playroom. But even that was contrasted, by its very location, by a delightful harvested store of counterfeits: the clue that sent the winners and losers alike puffing up the last stairs, and pulling up the dusty shades, contained a reference to Pandora's Box that led to the old toy-chest which, on being opened, proved to contain a number of beautifully wrapped and beribboned prizes, one for each player and so marked with his or her name. The grown-ups had thought of everything.

These minor treasures cast into curious relief the major one, smaller in size but, even from the heavy, black matte paper of its wrapping (with a single, silver crescent moon sealing the four points that had been brought tightly around behind it), let alone from its greater weight, obviously more precious and more intense. The wrapped object, wedged between the dollhouse walls, perfectly constituted the promised prize, but only until it was opened. For then the penumbra of indeterminacy that had enfolded the treasure ("—*And the winners will get to keep the treasure*" said the grown-up who explained the rules) was violently dispelled, and the wrapped, unknown prize suddenly became two specific objects, and could enter deep into the lives of the winning pair through the usual gateways of possession, use, misuse, and perhaps damage or loss.

On the other hand, when "The Prize" had not yet been destroyed, it could not be part of their lives in the usual sense. It could not be possessed: only the access to its interior could, and that itself was quickly consumed. As it lay there in its matrix or cradle of toy enclosure, though, it held its discoverers in a strange relation that transcended possession, that kept the package momentarily attached to their lives while yet remaining beyond them.

So you see that "the treasure" is not a simple matter, let alone the whole question of figurative treasure, like the irretrievable moment of joy and sorrow that was vouchsafed the north window of the morning room when one of the younger players, a girl of about twelve in a pale green blouse and slacks, her long hair bouncing gently off her back, took a sudden series of child-like skips as she raced past the outside of that window, on the lawn, a paper clue in her hand. If the window could be said to "remember," it would never forget the sight of the girl; but the feelings that were wrapped up in the moment of vision could never endure.

The Twin's Story

My twin brother and I had been placed in different families shortly after birth, and although I had known of his existence, we never met until we were both in our early thirties. I grew up in the city, he in the country, although the effects of this in our two natures were not what you might think. For by that time our cities had already become what they are today—had lost their cosmopolitan character and had become massed villages, enclosures rather than confluences. The country had lost its innocence, but of course had never acquired the generous skepticism, the joy in the multiplicities of life's versions, that the cities once engendered—wide as its exposure to nature was, the country afforded only a narrow window onto human variety.

Well, then. My brother and I, different as our circumstances were, finally met by some peculiar combination of chance and design. My parents—or rather, my foster parents, for my true mother and father had been killed in a grisly and meaningless accident a few months after my birth—had spoken of a twin brother who had been taken away by distant relatives. But they had so casually managed to dampen my natural curiosity, by means that I can now barely manage to understand, that the details of the question never seemed to matter. Perhaps I had been encouraged to feel that any attempt to discover or encounter this brother would end in disaster, or that it would be extraordinarily unseemly. In any event, I never felt much interest in pursuing the problem. But this did not prevent me from taking great comfort in the notion—even when I was very young—that there existed somewhere in the world a strange kind of completion of my body and my consciousness. Although I was apparently finished off—with no missing limbs, nor palpable deficiencies of

From *Partisan Review* 51 (1984–85). Written in 1982.

sense or metabolism or whatever that might need correction—I alone knew and felt that, actual encounter or proximity aside, an embodiment of the rest of me—rather than *more* of me—was part of the available universe, and that he—who and wherever he was—stood as some ultimately redemptive being for any missing element or quality of which even I might be unaware. I grew so used to the feeling of security to which this notion gave rise that I would leave it undisturbed even by meditation.

It was not until I was old enough not only to have put away childish things, but to have returned to them, as it were, in the way that certain fortunate adults can manage to do, that I could consider this sense I had of the Other one, and what it all might mean. In those days, I traveled for a notions manufacturer, visiting both wholesalers and chain retailers that did a large business. Driving at night, or in buses or airplanes on short hops, I would often look out into the distant darkness, moving and motionless both, as if searching it not for someone else possibly hidden there, but for a truth or an answer in another kind of hiding: What did my unknown twin brother correct in me? What incompleteness did he add to? Would there be some reciprocating defect in his nature that was redeemed in mine? It was only in the year in which I finally realized my defective property—which was purely and simply my uniqueness itself—that I encountered my brother in a bar in a small New England town.

Outside it was dark—a late fall evening—and dark within, but I had an immediate sense, as I saw from a booth a figure with its back toward me standing at the bar, that this was someone I knew. When he turned around to leave, I saw who indeed it was and walked up to him immediately, leaving him no time in which to be startled. I set out at once to explain myself—and, in a way, himself—to him. I discovered that although he knew that his parents had been adoptive, he was unaware of my existence. But our identical resemblances, my story, and reasonable inference after his initial shock and disbelief, combined during the course of the evening to convince him.

We had walked to his home, a small house in an older part of town (like me at the time, he was unmarried), and we sat quietly there, drinking and talking, until very late. From that night on, we saw each other at long but regular intervals, either in the city on weekends, or in the town where he lived and worked in the management of a mill. All this is, actually, unremarkable enough. Both of us had lost our foster parents and were without other relatives; we were both hardworking and solitary, both used to avoiding intimate friendships with the men of our acquaintance and to anything more than guarded, casual affairs with women. Neither of us was ready or willing to claim the other for a new-found and unsettling friendship, and our blood relationship—even this ultimate of those—could only be represented socially by improvisation.

For my part, my sense of completeness in another one remained undisturbed by the mere actuality of his presence. Given the banality of both our lives, an account of our subsequent relations might have remained banal as well. He never had the sense of completion that tinted even the darkest days of my life, and could barely understand what I meant on the one occasion at which I unwisely attempted to explain it. And, as I have said, his reality neither augmented nor diminished that feeling, nor would I allow it to alter my life in any other way. The fact of his existence was like that of a very important text, an explanation or commentary without which the text of my life would be unreadable; he himself was like a copy of the book, no less and no more.

Then one night he tried to kill me. Or rather, he came at me with what might have been murderous effects; the intent, if murderous itself, was not so much his as that of a drunken rage he had acquired and been unable to dispose of. We were both solitary but moderate drinkers; on our visits we would seldom go out, being unwilling to deal with the stares that adult twins seem to attract, and, even more, with the reflected sight of ourselves in store windows, or of the paired shadows whose sinister quality lay in their very innocence—they might have been shadows, for example, of any two men of roughly the same height. And so we would usually meet, eat, talk, and drink at his house or mine, and after a few years, this had become a ritual. I would know exactly, during the evening, how it would end; I could anticipate the quality of the air on the street outside his door, or the strange light in the corridor outside my apartment, the words we always spoke after an interval of silence: "Well, then"; and he would answer, "I guess so."

But that night he drank much more than usual, and grew

more and more silent between our brief exchanges. I felt uneasy, and since I had to leave very early the next morning for a long trip, I tried to bring the evening to an early close. The meeting was at my apartment, and I rose from my chair, walked to a table on which his trench coat lay folded, turned to where he was standing nearby and spoke:

"Well, then."

"No, not well at all, you bastard," he suddenly snarled and rushed at me with outstretched fists. I was so taken aback that defense against even this childish and ridiculously fragile assault was impossible for the moment. During that moment he reached me, battered me in the face, seized my neck, and started to choke me. Only after what was almost too long a time did outrage, terror, and disgust combine to fuel my awareness and strength. I finally struggled free, kicked him several times in the groin and stomach, got him to the floor, and pinned him there with my knees.

He groaned softly for a while and said nothing. He refused to answer my question about the meaning of his attack, or about anything else. Suddenly taken by a painful thought, I wrestled his wallet from his coat pocket, opened it up, and on an identification card I found there, saw among other facts listed "in case of accident," his blood type. It was not my own.

I shouted out something that started as a question and immediately dissolved into a cry of terror and dismay; then I ran from my apartment, scarcely bothering to shut the door behind me, raced down the stairs without waiting for the elevator, and rushed out into the street. Mindlessly distraught, I walked through drizzling rain without a coat, pushing through streets still busy with night traffic, and still occupied by scurrying pedestrians. When I returned home after an hour, he was gone, the door shut, and nothing disturbed within. I never saw him again.

The problem, of course, was mine, not his; and even after some months when I tried to check up on him, and found that he had quit his job, moved, and left no forwarding address, it did not change the situation. For there was no explanation he could have given me that would have helped. Naive acquiescence, designing guile, or whatever, motive seemed to me to have nothing to do with the truth of what had happened.

Nature produces doubles as well as twins, but cannot be

blamed for the first of these any more than for the second. Twinship is as much a learned as a given state, but one's relation to a double is totally of one's own making. I had quested, without being fully aware of how I was doing it, for a twin. But as in all significant quests, the goal and the final task, as well as many of the later intermediate stages, are invented by the searcher. It is not only that the nature and meaning of the task changes during the course of executing it. It is that the end gets reinvented during the later phases.

And so I had created my twin, but I had bungled somehow and ended up with a mere double, another person whose otherness from myself was so ordinary as to be trivial—someone with nothing to do with me, someone as meaningless as a namesake. There had been no significant change in my way of life while I still believed him to be my twin brother, nor were our lives together of any consequence. But the discovery of his existence, and the termination of his being my twin, were profound and catastrophic. In the latter instance, it was as if I had made a stone image and then broke it; but whether the breaking was to bring good luck or bad I was not to know. The first of these events put an end to a strangely muted but obsessive kind of search. The second instigated a very different kind of one, a search for no guerdon, a mission toward no ultimate showdown, whether of real or figurative battle, a recircling journey toward no home. It was rather a search whose sea-voyages and treks inland, whose bookings and arrangements, whose map readings and takings of stock, all occurred in the domain of questionings. Like some topological game requiring the player to move on a board through as many points as possible, this domain into which I had been thrust to live my moral life caused me to do so not by traversing the field, but to live among the questions and doubts that blossomed everywhere, wherever an answer fell.

But questions of the kind one would think might nag at me fell away long ago, questions about *him,* and what "actually" happened. The questions I live with are all about *me,* and about *it* (or everything else). And even what might appear to be a terminal or limiting question about all that (the years in which he was part of my life went by fifteen years ago)—What if he were not *your* double, but a double of some twin brother of yours, from whom you might have been separated, say, in infancy, a twin brother whom this person encountered once in the way he did you, a twin brother whom he either killed, or, more likely, caused to abandon him, and so forth?—even *that* question no longer looms up before me like a menacing indeterminacy along a forest road on a moonless night. It simply stands, like a funny rock formation at the far end of a field, more or less visible and more or less problematic in its possible figuration, depending upon the weather.

Terah's Idols

It is not in fact written in *Bereshit,* or Genesis, but only told in Midrash how Abraham smashed the idols in the house of his father, Terah, long before the time of his going forth. But the idols are not named, not even by the much later secret commentary on the story which points out that the idols, being too literal, had to be smashed, lest the figurative, the metaphoric, die in a tomb of stone. Yet a variant text of this commentary has recently been discovered that has no such reticence about the appearance of the idols. They were:

(1) *The Moon of Moons.* She had breasts shaped like the waxing and waning crescents, carved in bas-relief. Far below these, but centered between them, her full circle of hole shone out, shorn of its hairy brow, as if the double-convex slit had widened, over a month of months, into this opening of perfection, of emptiness, of wonder, and of nought. Her head, turned completely backward, presented a polished hemisphere that—depending upon one's sense of appropriateness—either gave no indication, or else totally revealed, the abominations associated with her worship. But it is maintained that her hole was wide enough to admit an adult head and shoulders.

(2) *The Ox-Person.* No amiably monstrous minotaur, this, with a huge horned head surmounting a proportionate and muscular man's body, in a travesty of normal completion. No indeed— a slow, fat, ex-frame, rudely but unmistakably cut with a choppy surface in high relief from an otherwise smooth and gleaming block of obsidian. Thrusting out of the area of its shoulders was the tiny head of a newborn infant, its mouth twisted in a howl of

From *Orim: A Jewish Journal at Yale* (1984). Written in 1982.

pain—the pain of its ill-assorted being, the pain of unwise composition, of the crude, early stages of blending and of one thing becoming another. The question it posed was of where divinity actually lay: was it in the height of head that could raise a figure of earth to the stars? or in the base of anything, bearing up whatever wretched head was being tortured by the dead weight of stony firmament? The carver, in this case, appears to have been in doubt about where he stood, as to where in the history of making images he came along.

(3) *The Pig.* Even priests of its cult kept their distance. Although relatively small in scale, this image must have looked too gross for household use. It had a curved knife—almost a sickle, it seemed—stuck into its fat neck, the pig having been carved with a slot in its reddish stone to receive the tiny bronze toy. No ceremony called for the removal or use of the knife; it seems to have been thrust into the stone throat of the pig only once, perhaps in consecration, and then never removed. The pig stood on a truncated, conical pillar of gray stone that shattered as easily as the god it bore, but with a more conventional sound; the image itself, when it was smashed, made a low, wet noise, as if of suction and of mud.

(4) *The House.* It was a model, but not in scale. We might think it grotesquely out of scale, in fact: the walls were as thick as the rooms they enclosed; the inner courtyard was left unfinished; the columns of the front door were far too small for the vast lintel they would have had, in the full scale of actuality, to support. With their typical form (elaborate, decorated bases, but no capitals at all), these columns seemed like mere rods poking into the flat stone above them. The House rested on a base, itself supported by a piece of freestanding column, in normal scale and rising just above human height; it may have come from just the sort of house whose miniature and misshapen representation it bore. A depression, basinlike, was cut into the lower part of the column, above the base, to receive the tears of the worshiper.

(5) *The Lump.* It was an inexplicably ordinary-looking lump of rock, with no magnetic or flintlike properties, containing no

ores or visible crystals. It stood furthest away from the Moon of Moons. The deep mark of a single chisel cut on its bottom was invisible, but attested to its maker's skill. It seems to have been the newest of all the idols.

(6) *The Cup.* Not in itself the sacred image, but a ritual container for the water within it, which was. Every week it was refilled to the top, to compensate for evaporation, from some other source that could not be used again until six months had gone by.

(7) *The Seven.* Seven tiny pillars, each with a flat, empty top, that resisted even the late rage of Abraham's destruction, refused to break, and had to be carried, one by one in cuddling arms, to a nearby chasm and flung into the abyss. They crashed into the water at its bottom but whether they broke on the rocks deep below the surface, or whether they lie there still, is not known.

It was these that Abraham—before his name had been expanded from Abram—destroyed with, of course, no hint of compassion, and it was for these that he substituted nothing.

In Ancient Days

One thing should be made clear at the outset: the ancient society in which the events I shall recount took place was unique in its laws of property and, particularly, in its system of slaveholding.

We have been taught to find something deeply contingent about the grandeur of antiquities that were assembled by the toil of slaves—not so much a tarnished beauty as an invisible inner fault that we cannot perceive, but nonetheless know to be there. We wish to think of it—although by reason of no laws of mechanics, as a structural defect. Time has built ruins by more means than those of obvious destruction, for it has brought into being such vast concerns as ours for the qualities of human labor and freedom, outrage at generations of toil in order that the Gods of Others might be embodied in space and stone. This has been an almost geological evolution: from out of the milky liquid of an earlier age in which our faith lay suspended or, even more unaccountably, it is as if clear water could dry up and leave jagged rock in its place. Thus the major ruin appears when beauty is put into disappointing shadow by an almost opaque moral presence that has crystallized only in time.

To tell of these people and their peculiar institution is not, then, so much to deal with their habit of distributing all slaves— bought, conquered, or born in captivity (after the age of thirteen)—equally among male and female adults in the population. Rather it is to confront this single, terrifying fact: there could be no manumission. Slaves, however acquired, could not be freed under any circumstances, not by any law of the society or ancient custom, but by reason of a law of nature itself. Long before the time of which I write, it had been determined that

From *Moment* 1 (1982).

any slave, set free by his or her owner, would die within a few days. Whether of some ordinary or rare illness; whether by some grotesque but unavoidable accident, such as one involving a huge, falling stone; whether by the apparent result of a dazzled condition in which the victim would step calmly into a deep cistern or climb to a snowy height and fall asleep—in any event, nature did not suffer a freed slave to live.

The profound and complex cast that this circumstance bestowed upon the owner-slave relation, manifested in custom as well as in law, may be imagined. What is more remarkable is the way these complexities were reflected in these people's more general habits of ownership. Their slaves were to them, variously according to the imaginative capacities of the owners, as pets, blood relatives, or even embodied presences of one's sense of life in the world, to lose a grip on which would be death. The word for "slave" in their language was derived from the root for "word," although their writers seemed not generally to be aware of this. But these strange modes of possession of other people affected all other property as well: land, houses, cloth, pots, weapons, harps, drums, scrolls, and carved representations of their pleasures and sorrows—these people appear to have had no gods. So that nobody could be said to "use" a tool in the sense that we do; for example: just as their intimate, responsible, life-maintaining relations to their slaves prevented them from "using" slaves like things or livestock—or even, by extension, from brutalizing themselves by metaphorically "using," as we say, other citizens—so something of this extended to any place or thing to which this equivalent of our pronoun *my* could be suffixed. (This may be misleading, though, for some grammarians deny that their language had anything like a possessive case.) They dwelt with—not merely in—their places. Their useful objects had a kind of life with them, so that even the most humdrum of activities, such as taking inventory of jugs of oil or wine, mending a sandal or a sail, reminding a child for the fortieth time that earthenware can break, all took place, outdoors or in, in a kind of holy place, sanctified by the mutual touch of human life and this figurative being of place and thing. Even a storage closet was like the studio of a brooding painter of our day, every hammer a violinist's dearest Amati. People lived in companionate marriage with their possessions.

Well, then. One bright morning, a day whose sky and gently moving air would dispel the memory, let alone the presence, of anything like mystery, on a hill that overlooked the somewhat distant marketplace of the city, a young man . . .

From the Memoirs of
an Administrator

1.

You see, it was because one's rights in property were more assiduously protected, under the Former System, than one's rights to and in one's person, that we had to change everything. We took the property away and tried to share the Things as well as we could. And to protect our New Way of doing all that, we had to get everyone to abandon one's last residue of property, his or her person. For it was the person to which that anarchic pronoun *my* continued to be affixed (with all of the arrogance of a robber baron, waving his arm in a gesture that people like ourselves could only employ dismissively, but that he must needs use to designate the extent of his holdings). So that to prevent property from creeping back, like poor second-growth vegetation, into the centers of our lives, we had to do something about the Self.

This was simple enough to manage, but perhaps it has gone on working for so long because of one bold stroke, executed at the outset. After much speculation, planning, and experiment, we instituted the practice of allowing that there was, indeed, one human—but nonproprietary—right, that of suicide. Its exercise was permitted, in an act of official recognition accompanied by three days of ceremony, instruction, and national festivity. But the licensing never seemed to have affected the actual suicide rate one way or another. We knew that this would be the case. The exercise of freedom was too dearly bought, it seems, for there to be much of a demand for it. Who can tell us that this was unfair? Unjust?

From *Commentary* (September 1981).

2.

At bottom, the problem has been one of the inequities of luck; the very random pattern of its distribution makes that uneven distribution more of a conferring of privilege, not less of one. Infested with Temples of Fortune, even the Just City would develop its priests and its powers. In order to prevent this, we shall have to institute the final state of fairness: all lives will be prolonged, by whatever heroic medical approaches are necessary, until three score and ten; all will thereupon be terminated, whether the citizen in question has been dependent upon these means, or hale and hearty without them. This will considerably reduce the seed-ground of future injustice. Life will be allotted fairly to everyone; the "freedom" to live past a certain age will soon become as dubious a notion as what—even in our time—only a fool could call the "liberty" of dying young. Moreover, such a plan would do away, once and for all, with that plaguey and inconvenient fiction called Fortune, a force that our theories of justice have demystified and sought to extinguish.

3.

The fair, equitable distribution of pain—that was another matter entirely. Our earliest planners had realized that pleasure would surely take care of itself: even back in the former days of privacy and unequal possession, pleasure redistributed itself more efficiently than wealth. Even—indeed, particularly—with no desire to share it, the suffusing joy experienced by one person would lead inevitably to someone else's delight, and so on. (Although the mathematical description of the stochastic processes involved in the distributions made writing equations for them almost impossible.) Pleasure could, under any social circumstances, make its way through the world. But the manner in which we had always hoarded up our own pain seemed a horrible reciprocal of this. For the greater the desire there was, under the old system, to unburden oneself of the private possession of pain—the more strident and desperate the means people adopted to share pain by calling attention to their own, by demanding that it be pieced out—the less anyone else would and could have access to it. The political economy of pain remained a troublesome riddle.

For the only solution we could devise dissolved not only the problem but what was to be shared as well. By implanting transmitter-receptors in all infants at birth, every impulse passing through anyone's pain centers would be instantaneously broadcast, as by the winnowing wind, at a frequency to which everyone would be tuned. Willy-nilly, one's pain would be universally shared. But because of inevitable engineering problems—the painful impulses themselves being employed for power supply, and thereby being diffused along with the message of hurt they carried—the pain could never, after all, be fairly distributed. For when parceled out, each receptor's quantum of feeling would fall far below any perceptible threshold. (Such a portion of suffering would have no more presence, practically speaking, than, say, the finite but meaninglessly small gravitational force of the red star Antares upon our bodies from its mindlessly large distance.) There are about 150 million of us under the present administration; and yet there is no bearable human pain—none known that would not extinguish itself by causing immediate traumatic death—that augments the lowest perceptible level by more than a factor of a mere thousand. 1.5×10^{-9} of even the worst toothache could not be shared, nor could the exhaustion of loss: they would simply vanish into the world.

So that the whole project had to be abandoned. There was no way of parceling out physical or moral suffering without thereby immediately destroying its effects (and what, after all, is pain but our feeling of it?). It seemed somehow obscene to put into effect a plan that would be truly guilty of the otherwise false and groundless charges usually and shrilly leveled against our collectivizations of property and opportunity—that they vanished when broadly distributed. What could we do? This was surely one of our greatest failures.

II

Poetic Translation

Found in Translation

Translating the Classics

> But nothing's lost. Or else: all is translation
> And every bit of us is lost in it
> (Or found . . .
>
> —James Merrill, "Lost in Translation"

My subject is such that I must immediately acknowledge some out-
standing precursors, such wonderful books as Reuben Brower's
book on Pope, and the collection of essays he edited called *On
Translation; The Craft and Context of Translation* edited by the late
William Arrowsmith and Roger Shattuck; and that splendid vol-
ume *The Art of Translation* edited by Professor Warren. My specific
title is a phrase antithetical to what is meant in the saying attrib-
uted to Robert Frost that poetry is what gets lost in translation.
And it is that specifically which I'll concern myself with in much
of these remarks. But the phrase can mean something else, af-
fecting broader issues of culture, and I should really go into that
first. When the classics themselves are lost in their original
tongues—literacy being confined, however sophisticated it is, to
vernaculars—they can, and have continued to be, found again in
their translated versions.

This may be an obvious point, but it is one continually worth
reexamination, because what it is that is actually "found" changes
so much, and because the very process of searching changes un-
der the pressure of awareness of its own history, like poetry itself.
The very small Latin and shockingly less Greek that I had ac-
quired halfway through college was not there to serve me when,
as a freshman, I was exposed to a very canonically "classical"

From *Annals of Scholarship* 11, no. 3 (winter 1997); read, in shorter
form, at an MLA session on the classics and modern literature, Decem-
ber 1993.

notion of "the classics" (classical literature having a privileged place in the canon because the further back you go along the cable of the canonical, the less it tends to fray). Nevertheless, without translation my classmates and I would never have been able to find Homer, Herodotus, Thucydides, four plus by each of the tragedians and by Aristophanes, Aristotle's *Poetics, The Apology, The Symposium,* and at least Francis Cornford's version of *The Republic,* the *Nichomachean Ethics* and the first books of the *Politics,* Lucretius, Virgil and not Ovid—alas, the *Metamorphoses* was not a Columbia–Chicago–St. John's Great Book, but only became one for me later, as a neoteric poet—but Augustine's *Confessions.* I later became acquainted with at least passages from most of these in the original. Still, these were all read in translation, albeit with knowledgeable glossing from the instructors about the sorts of things that were being lost in the process of our being able to find the works themselves.

Literary works can of course be translated "for" readers who can't read the original, and also for readers who will even be expected to. One thinks of Elizabethan translators of Greek works and of Latin ones in this connection. More English readers in the eighteenth and nineteenth centuries could be counted on to have some Virgil and Horace by heart than to have Homer, and that may be why the history of Homeric translation in English is even more of a paradigm of the history of poetry in English generally than is the array of versions of Virgil. Thus readers find the original works in some translations, but in others (particularly of poetry, where the losses, incidentally, are greatest) there are all sorts of figurative findings.

We must acknowledge that there are some ambiguities in the terms we are invoking. Of these, the word *translation* probably presents the fewest difficulties. We may follow Dryden's differentiations of *metaphrase*—or what he called "turning an author word by word and line by line, from one language into another"—from *paraphrase,* or translation with latitude ... the author's "words not so strictly followed as his sense; and that too is admitted to be amplified, but not altered." Finally there is *imitation*—"taking only some hints from the original" (this last he likens musically to divisions on a ground). Modern verse translation, more sophisticated about theory of language, would want to argue that it is often impossible to achieve metaphrase without some paraphrase, and that certain "untranslatable" elements in any passage or work have indeed to be rendered through imitation. I think here of metrical schemes and the rhythmic events occurring within their framework, lost puns, necessary displacements or analogues of phonological patterns like assonance and alliteration, and so forth. And it may be apparent from this observation that I shall be addressing the matter of poetic translation primarily here.

As for "classics," on the one hand, it is presumed that those of classical antiquity are implied, although today we find that Tennyson might as well be writing in a learned language for many college students who had never memorized any verse at school, nor read any periodic prose, for that matter. And on the other hand, we might want to say that Elizabethan poetry and Milton were classical for Keats. In Sir Frank Kermode's fine little book *The Classic,* which treats these questions profoundly and broadly, we are reminded that it is a late author, Aulus Gellius, who first uses the term. But short of warning that Stendahl's infamous definition of a classic as "what gave great pleasure to our great-grandfathers and which we can't pretend doesn't make us yawn" clearly refers to the wrong kind of stuffy neoclassic, I shall leave the matter of the classical vs. the neoclassical alone. It is harder to decide which sense of "modern" to address: Sappho, Theocritus, and Callimachus could all be thought of as revisionary modernists; the major modernist might be St. Paul. But all these were "modernisms" too: the Renaissance, later neoclassicism, romantic Hellenism (so different in German and in English because of the intervening pantheon of Shakespeare, Spenser, and Milton, neoteric classics in their own right), or twentieth-century high modernism (say, ca. 1922).

There is a wide range of instances of such different scales, and one scarcely knows where to begin. Broader modernity (the *quattrocento* and after, perhaps) has propounded successively differing constructions of, attitudes toward, reasons and modes for preserving and even differently understood textual economies of gain and loss—the necessary trade-offs of all writing. For a postenlightenment secular culture, translations of "the classics" form a parallel to the vernacular Scriptures and the liturgy of the Reformation. And, to choose an instance from Anglo-American high literary modernism, Joyce's *Ulysses* reminds us that the *Odyssey*, as the original quest-epic, anticipates all quest romances and all of the revisions of subsequent modernisms, whereas the *Iliad* does not: the poem that begins with the man, "Andra," humanely invites such revision, whereas the poem that begins in anger, "Mênin," almost angrily refuses it, which is partly why moderns prefer the first six books of the *Aeneid*.

As far as poetry goes, the classical languages can lose things in themselves. Hebrew was kept alive liturgically and interpretively after Aramaic, Greek, Romance languages, Judaeo-German, and other tongues displaced it as a vernacular. As far as poetry goes, the classical languages can lose things in themselves. Hebrew was kept alive liturgically and interpretively after Aramaic, Greek, Romance languages, Judaeo-German, and other tongues displaced it as a vernacular. But issues of the actual rhythm in Hebrew verse were swamped by musical and other changes. English literature faced the special issue of Latin in a non-Catholic country over almost four centuries—particularly the great-sound-shifted pronunciation, drilled on weekdays into the heads of the educated minority, as opposed to the church Latin intoned in the mass for a wider continental reception.

There are of course the findings of mythography. In one sense, the classics are always being "gothicized"—as a disapproving voice in Hawthorne's *A Wonder Book*, objecting to the story-teller's New England Spenserizings of an Ovidian fable, put it—in some way or another. Scholars think immediately of the mass of medieval and renaissance mythography and of all the secular sermons preached and inscribed in classical mythology. But ad hoc mythography, at least for poets, continues up through the modern period, even if it entails a debunking of all previous mythographic modes. Even the recovery and presentation of the Ur may, Schliemann-like, dig down through the Homeric city in an attempt to avoid the Hellenistic ones. And even that project is its own, post-Fraserian sort of "gothicizing." Indeed, one definition of a classic may be that it constitutes a set of occasions for gothicizing. These frequently lead to moments of marvelous, post-renaissance *imitation,* not to speak of strong revisionary readings. I think here not so much of the imprinting of a new element of a translated story into the substrate of the original (for example, the fact that it is Rousseau, not Ovid, who names Pygmalion's creature Galatea), as of certain modernist moments. Thus, as opposed to French neoclassicisms in drama, from Corneille and Racine through Giraudoux (*La Guerre de Troie n'aura pas lieu* and particularly *Electre*), we must consider that great work of modernism, Jean Cocteau's film *Orphée* as major mythographic revision of an English Renaissance sort (that the French Renaissance never really grappled with, perhaps). But in this regard, I am reminded how the poetic thought of later modernism depends so much on a revision of the received translation of *mimesis*—particularly in versions of Aristotle's *Poetics*—as "imitation," and privileges instead *"representation,"* a kind of conceptual reformation that acknowledges greater authenticity for the fictive object.

For literate and literarily sophisticated younger readers (of a kind that used to be more in evidence), an encounter with a classical text means finding that topoi or tags had not always been free-floating currency. The classical equivalent of the child who reported, on seeing her first Shakespearean play, that it was full of quotations, is a more complex matter. But it still has the quality of discovering the source of all the many rivulets one had always known, and always thought to have arisen independently in the landscape. Yet for various eras of "modern" poetry there are hundreds of examples of the way tags—Dawn's rosy dactyls, Sappho's freezing and burning at once—can become, like the plucked flower of the moment in Horace's *carpe diem*—topoi in the sixteenth and seventeenth centuries. It is instructive to see what happens when two early-seventeenth-century poets translate— somewhere between Dryden's *paraphrase* and *imitation*—the same celebrated lines of Catullus V, the *"Vivamus mea Lesbia, atque amemus."* Jonson's version recontextualizes the poem as a dramatic song in *Volpone:*

> Come, my Celia, let us prove
> While we may the sports of love.
> Time will not be ours forever
> He at length our goods will sever.
> Spend not then his gifts in vain:
> Suns that set may rise again,
> But if once we lose this light,
> 'Tis with us perpetual night . . .
> *[nox est perpetua una dormienda]*

But Jonson's song goes off even more into the Horatian *carpe diem*, finally ending up with the assurance that there's nothing wrong with adultery except getting caught at it, not there in the Catullus at all:

> 'Tis no sin love's sweets to steal,
> But the sweet theft to reveal,
> To be taken, to be seen:
> These have crimes accounted been.

Thomas Campion more faithfully translates Catullus in a song of his:

> My sweetest Lesbia, let us live and love,
> And, though the sager sort our deeds reprove,
> Let us not weigh them. Heaven's great lamps do dive
> Into their west, and straight again revive.
> But soon as once is set our light,
> Then must we sleep one eve-during night.
> *[nobis cum semel occidit brevis lux*
> *nox est perpetua una dormienda]*

But what Campion "finds" in Catullus's perpetual sleep of night is a fine and flexible refrain for a strophic lyric. In its successive stanzas, the phrase delicately modulates as a result of its application to Campion's new material. In stanza 2, it is the fools who would make war, not love who "live and waste their little light. / And seek with pain their ever-during night." In the final strophe, the speaker asks that, when he dies, no emblems of mourning be placed on his tomb, but that, instead, it be graced by couples making love; and he adjures his own lover,

> And, Lesbia, close up thou my little light,
> And crown with love my ever-during night.

He almost turns the sleep of death into an unending *nuit d'amour*.

Then there is the matter of what I might call metrical grounding. By this I mean not so much the construction of analogues of classical formal structures for vernacular poetry (e.g., the ill-fated struggle to adapt classical scansion to English verse in the later sixteenth century about which Derek Attridge has written so well), but rather what particular poets learn from the requirements of poetic translation. The earl of Surrey finds—discovers, reinvents (it having been lost except in Scots after Chaucer)— English blank verse in his wonderful translation of part of the *Aeneid,* although it would take the intervention of Milton before English translations could think of doing Virgil that way again. Goethe in the fifth of his Roman Elegies finds himself enthused by the very ground itself: *"Nun empfind ich mich nun auf klassischem Boden begeistert; / Vor- und Mitwelt spricht lauter und reizender mir"* [Here on classical ground I feel myself to be enraptured / Past and Present speak clearer, more charming to me]. But we almost feel that the *Boden,* the ground, is composed not of Roman road but of the accentual elegiac couplets themselves. Indeed, in some celebrated lines halfway through this delightful little poem, the classical measures are given not only voice, but touch. He is speaking now of his Roman girlfriend: *"Oftmals hab ich auch schon in ihren Armen gedichtet / Und des Hexameters Mass leise mit fingernder Hand / Ihr auf den Rücken gezählt"* [Often have I even written poems in her arms, and / Gently counted out hexameters' measures with five / Fingers upon her back] although he reaches across from the pentameter line to do so.

But this very romantic classical ground got pounded upon again in English revision, when W. H. Auden could complete the cycle of adaptations of the alcaic strophe, from Greek to Latin, to German accentual finally to a form of Marianne Moore's pure syllabics in his elegy for Freud, and in a poem called "The Dark Years," strophes of two lines of eleven syllables, followed by one of nine and then one of ten. (This accounts, incidentally, for his peculiar indentation pattern there—not with the nine-syllable alcaic indented once, and the following lesser alcaic twice, but just the reverse, respectively shorter lines based on absolute syllable count.) And if a mere typographic convention—itself based on modern textual practice—seems too trivial for this matter of modern *version,* one might consider for a moment the fascinating device, which I have noted elsewhere, that is employed by Ben Jonson in the 1616 folio edition of his *Works.* The earlier rhymed fourteener couplets that Arthur Golding had used for Ovid's—and Chapman for the *Iliad*'s—hexameters was being canonically displaced by English rhymed pentameter couplets. Yet Marlowe had in 1590 turned Ovid's *Amores* into those couplets as well, thus losing the joke, at the opening, about the elegiac couplet form in which they are written—Ovid says that he was planning to write of *"Arma . . . violentaque bella"* [arms, and the violences of war] in matter suited to the meter *["gravi numero . . . materia convenient modis"]*, and that his second line was equal in length to his first, when Cupid, laughing, stole one foot away (from the second line—Ovid thus reinvents the elegiac couplet as the result of erotic prank). Jonson, scrupulously concerned to make clear that the English couplet translates two classical meters, indents the second line—although of equal length, of course—of his couplets when they are to be elegiac—used in his epigrams; and yet in the one instance in the 1616 folio of his nondramatic verse in which they are to stand—as truly heroic couplets—for hexameters, in a brief mock-epic called *The Fabulous Voyage,* they are printed flush left (as are the couplets translating Horace's *Ars Poetica* in the 1640 folio). So Jonson finds "in" the always puzzling problem of not losing poetic form, either in its emblematic, genre-defining status or, more subtly and profoundly, in its ability to generate various kinds of rhythmic activity, an array of analogous uses for the English couplet—for narrative, epigram, satire, epistle.

And so, for example, for the purely modern reader, the question of Latin hendecasyllabics (as opposed to the word more loosely applied to the canonical Italian line) in vernacular poetry might seem inane. But Robert Frost employs it, with subtle allusion to its classical modality, in that wonderful and enigmatic poem "For Once, Then, Something." Nowhere is the meter alluded to in the poem, which is not quite a sonnet, but rather fifteen lines of unrhymed five-beat verse with a stressed analogue of the Latin meter. It begins as you'll remember:

> Others taunt me with having knelt at well-curbs
> Always wrong to the light, so never seeing
> Deeper down in the well than where the water
> Gives me back in a shining surface picture
> Me myself in the summer heaven, godlike . . .

The poem's deep epistemological agenda must be introduced by an implicit counterreproach to those who mock him for his falling not into the water, but into the error of Narcissus and of Milton's Eve. But the matter of taunt and reproach remain, even later in the poem when ripples of wave disturb the mirroring surface of the well, and "Water came to rebuke the too clear water." It is the hendecasyllabic as Catullus's melody of taunt and rebuke that is being invoked here, but troped, turned, revised from the more literally Catullan use of it by Robert Bridges, in his "To Catullus," with its splendid final line about how neither of "those two pretty Laureates of England" can hold a candle to Catullus, "Not Alfred Tennyson nor Alfred Austin," where the wonderful bathetic fall from the higher to the lower Alfred follows the given cadence of the line, and somehow elicits its essentially biting character. But Bridges was a heavy, and Frost an ulterior, classicist, and, like Pope, the corpus of classical texts that in translation arise in fragments of echo and allusion in his work includes Milton along with Homer and Virgil. It might also be said that he found something of his own voice in it, at least once.

As a recent instance of the strength of this metrical grounding, I might cite that of the superb contemporary Canadian poet Daryl Hine's verse letter to Theocritus. In it, the accentual hexameters—the gift of German romantic verse to English poetry—carry him on past his task into nearly 650 lines, in re the subsequent history of pastoral that ranks for me with studies by Empson and Rosenmeyer as being crucial to the understanding of the life of the mode in poetic modernity. Yet we could hardly call his use of them either neoclassic or even neoromantic.

But there is not room in these brief and casual observations for more detail. I should rather close with a more general question than that of what writers find or discover about their own language in the mirroring surface of another. Speaking from the cusp of this same twentieth-century modernism, Ezra Pound's persona in the first of the Hugh Selwyn Mauberley poems, "E.P. Ode Pour l'Election de Son Sepulchre" prefers "mendacities" to "the classics in paraphrase." Given the swirl of ambivalences marking that poem, I can ascribe neither that preference, nor an antipathy to that preference, to such a paraphraser of the classics as Pound himself. At a later moment, the same poet inadvertently raises my final question here:

> The thought of what America would be like
> If the Classics had a wide circulation
>   Troubles my sleep . . .
>
>   (*Little Review*, March 1918)

So commences Ezra Pound's redundantly repetitive satirical blast. Its thrust is quite ambiguous, itself perhaps troubled by bad faith. The decidedly un-Franciscan "Cantico del Sole" was apparently precipitated by a ruling of Judge Learned Hand. In arguing that an issue of the *Little Review* seized by postal authorities had First Amendment protection, he mentioned "numerous really great writings" that escape such seizure "only because they come within the term 'classics,' which means, for the purpose of application of the stature, that they are ordinarily immune from interference, because they have the sanction of age and fame and usually appeal to a comparatively limited number of readers." (Pound sneeringly referred to Judge Hand's "opinion" in inverted commas, as if the purely technical term for a genre of judicial writing were somehow inauthentic, a very cheap shot indeed.)

What really could have troubled Pound's sleep? The notion that if the classics had a wider circulation it would have to be in debased form? (Did he foresee *Classic Comics*?—He could never imagine a time when *Classic Comics* would seem Teubner editions in a world of young persons imprisoned in MTV.) Ezra Pound's sleep may indeed also have been troubled by bad faith with respect to the real problems of democratic education and how the excellent and noble builds upon—and thereby must not scorn too much—the vulgar. This is not a matter for discussion here. But the thought of what America is like, with not very much being suffered to have wide circulation except what is doomed by fashion to be forgotten in a few months; with practically no shared texts nor even songs that one might count on in a college class today—and I include here anecdotes from history (no longer taught much in the schools), scripture, mythology even "in paraphrase" of a puerile kind—with so little chance for even the most highly educated of students and younger teachers to experience and practice that fine range of modes of irony deployed by allusion in writing or speech; when these do not trouble my sleep in themselves, it is only because I am kept awake by the general condition of our culture in which this plays a strangely mixed role of symptom and debilitating vector. In a world in which there is nothing to try to translate yet again, getting it even better, contemporary originality may be that much harder to discover.

Circe's Children
Translating La Fontaine

Circe, the first satirist, turned men into the animals they "really" were; she made Odysseus's sailors into pigs, and Odysseus himself, but for the intervention of Hermes, a fox, or so Hawthorne suggested. Thus she invented one mode in which moral indignation has operated ever since, distorting the physical representation of people and their commodities in order to render correctly their usually hidden moral nature. She also thereby first allowed for the art of the animal fabulist, and so was, in a sense, the Muse of Aesop. Anecdotal stories of animals endowed with human speech who seem, by virtue of the traces of Circe's magic, to represent human qualities go back as far as Hesiod and Archilochus in early Greek poetry. We associate such stories with the name of Aesop, a slave probably living on Samos in the sixth century B.C.E., but "Aesop" comes to designate the canonical author of fables written down only later by others, much like "Moses" or "Homer."

The Greek word for "fable" (from latin *fabula*) is the familiar *mythos,* although what we generally speak of as Greek mythology refers to the cycles of stories about gods and heroes. A second-century A.D. rhetorician, Theon, defined fable as *logos pseudês eikonidzôn alêtheian,* "a false story picturing the truth," the story being anything from a telling metaphor to a long narration. (This seems remarkably unspecific to us, given that this is what we mean by parable, or even proverb and, indeed, by poetry gener-

---

Review-essay of *Fifty Fables of La Fontaine,* translated by Norman R. Shapiro (University of Illinois Press, 1988) and *The Complete Fables of Jean de la Fontaine,* edited by Norman B. Spector (Northwestern University Press, 1988). From *New Republic,* May 29, 1989.

ally.) The Aesopian stories, whether strictly of animals or other sorts of parable, were in prose. Versifying them, though, was apparently an early practice: Socrates in prison awaiting the execution of his sentence, Plato tells us in the *Phaedo,* not only propounded an Aesopian fable of his own (about how God, unable to reconcile the continual strife of pleasure and pain, fastened their heads together—thus when one of them comes, the other follows), but also, following the intimations of a dream to compose something, took some fables of Aesop that he knew and turned them into verse.

And so it is not surprising that the earliest Aesopian fables that we have are in verse. Horace, for example, has a speaker in one of his satires tell the familiar story of the country mouse and the city mouse, and versified collections in Latin by Phaedrus, in the early first century C.E., and slightly later, in Greek by Babrius, were themselves imitated and paraphrased in prose and verse, and so known in various collections in the Middle Ages. Chaucer tells and retells fables, and an elaborate version of one of them, in "The Nun's Priest's Tale," is one of the world's great masterpieces of profound comic vision. The Aesopian fable of the stomach and the limbs is retold tellingly and with powerful political consequences by Menenius in Plutarch's life of Coriolanus and, more profoundly and elaborately, in Shakespeare's play; and there are Aesopian fables, whether specifically of the animal sort or not, in much Renaissance poetry.

But just as the Greek myths in the Hellenistic handbooks were transformed, juxtaposed, intertwined, and brought to an amazing life of meaning and feeling by the poetry of Ovid, so the fables were totally transformed for us by Jean de La Fontaine in the seventeenth century. His great collection of some 250 fables in twelve books was published in three parts: the first six books in l668, five more ten years later, and a twelfth volume in l694, the year before he died. This rounded out an epical enterprise (there were twelve books in Virgil's *Aeneid*) that is half-signaled in the opening line of La Fontaine's dedicatory poem to the Dauphin: *"Je chante les héros dont Esope est le père"*—"I sing the heroes whose father is Aesop." (La Fontaine's gifts as a neoclassical poet are apparent in his lovely poem *Adonis,* about which Paul Valéry wrote a fine and central essay; he also invented the intriguing form of the *rondeau redoublé,* a mode that spins refrains out of its first quatrain.)

La Fontaine's collection contains fables of a variety of types drawn from a variety of sources (including those of the Indian fabulist Bidpai). The ones most familiar to English-speaking readers are perhaps those of the animal fables most often retold in other forms, or which became proverbial in themselves (the "sour grapes" of *Le Renard et les Raisins,* the fox and the grapes), or which, when most educated people learned French, used to be memorized at school (*Maître Corbeau, sur un arbre perché, / Tenait en son bec un fromage,* etc.). But there are many other sorts as well: etiological fables like the one Socrates proposed about pleasure and pain (*L'Amour la Folie* is a splendid one of these), or poems of wittily revisionary mythography, like the one on what happened to the Goddess Discord after the Homeric fable got through with her, which are rooted in traditions of Renaissance poetry. Stories of that sort contain their own moralizations, and, like the one about Love and Folly to be discussed further on, need no "application," as a concluding "moral" or interpretation was called in Renaissance storytelling.

But it is in the beast-fables that La Fontaine's moral and poetic thought interfuse in another way. We cannot be sure, when we hear a story about an ant and a grasshopper, for example, what is going to be talked about: could it be a fable of the Imagination, the grasshopper taking great leaps as a sort of insect Pegasus, while the drudging life of the ant permits it to be conscious of nothing more in the world than its burden, its task, its duty? That would, at any rate, be the grasshopper's story (or if *cigale* is more accurately translated as "cicada," then it's more a matter of singing, or fiddling, than jumping). But it is with the prudence of the ant that the Aesopian tradition has always sided, and that has had the last word.

It is only through the creatures' discourse—by means of the relation between the arguments they offer and their habits, natures, and interests in the matter at hand—that the moral is deployed. La Fontaine carries this much further than prior fabulists had ever done, for discourse is the substance of his animal world. "Natural" characteristics (or, rather, Circean, as opposed to zoologically defined ones) play a good part in La Fontaine's world—foxes *are* foxy, after all, cats never come off as much more than con men, and so on.

But the fictional power of these fables derives from two paradoxically opposed elements, a kind of "realism" for which the poet is celebrated (his animals are variously peasants, bourgeois, nobility, rather than emblematic or heraldic creatures) and, on the other hand, the mythical matter of there being any discourse at all. In the epilogue to book 11, the poet acknowledges the power of his own fiction by insisting, with a significant rhyme on *vers/univers* that unites two senses of "creation,"

> *Car tout parle dans l'univers;*
> *Il n'est rien qui n'ait son langage:*
> *Plus éloquents chez eux qu'ils ne sont dans mes vers,*
> *Si ceux que j'introduis me trouvent peu fidèle,*
> *Si mon oeuvre n'est pas assez mon modèle,*
> *J'ai du moins ouvert le chemin.*

[For everything speaks throughout creation—nothing is without its language; if, more eloquent at home than in my lines, those I present find me less than true to them—if my work isn't a good enough model, I've at least opened up a way.]

But by "nothing is without its language," he does not mean what a naturalist would, but rather, as a poet, that he can make them say anything believably, and thus make moral discourse itself believable. As one commentator (Francis Duke) has so well put it, "La Fontaine is exquisitely aware of the relation of the speech of animals to the metaphor of the animals as man, whose proudest attribute is speech with words." A modern schoolboy's joke is apposite here, in that it pointedly deconstructs just this one crucial aspect of beast-fable: it is the one about a horse and a cow engaged in a contentious argument, until a little dog that had been listening in silence suddenly intrudes by pointing out where a resolution lay, at which point horse and cow, shocked, both say to each other at once, "Look! A talking dog!!!" That the animals talk so well, and so humanly, runs along in counterpoint to the general Circean moral of all fabling, that people have animal natures usually hidden by language, custom, society, etc. These two notions entwined together make for the basis of La

Fontaine's poetic world; and whether in the language of dialogue among the creatures, in the wonderfully flexible modes of narration, or in the whole range of tones that he adopts in his prefaced or appended moral applications—frequently these have as much archness, plainness, high diction, or casual wisdom as any of his animals, the *"acteurs de mon ouvrage,"* as he calls them.

La Fontaine's morals are not easily classifiable. His stories can take Stoic or Epicurean positions in turn, and speak variously as it were for ants and grasshoppers. He is of the age of Molière rather than of Voltaire, and his pragmatic naturalism and (as directly expressed in the verse essay serving as epilogue to book 9) strongly anti-Cartesian views are accompanied by a clearly manifested love both of narrative and of his own characters, creating themselves through spoken language rather than, for the most part, by etiological myth.

The third-century A.D. Philostratus, in one of his *eikones* or descriptions of imaginary pictures, shows the Fables gathering "around Aesop, being fond of him because he devotes himself to them. . . . And Aesop, methinks, is weaving some fable; at any rate his smile and his eyes fixed on the ground indicate this." This looks like La Fontaine, with his eyes fixed on his page, and his ear attuned to the two harmonies of human speech in all its variety, and the immense resources of formal verse. This seems more appropriate as a visualization of the spirit of the fabulist than the fantastic labyrinth built at Versailles, in the smaller park, in 1677, which contained thirty-nine remarkable hydraulic statuary groups of Aesopian fables, in which jets of water spurted or spewed from the mouth of each animal in a representation of speech (the machinery for pumping enough water from the Seine to operate these cost the equivalent of tens of millions of dollars). At the entrance to the labyrinth stood statues of Aesop and, of course, Cupid (as Ariadne, holding in *his* hand the ball of thread as a guide to the way out of the maze—most poets would want to create some other figure holding the guide through Cupid's maze). But just as Renaissance poetry, viewing the ruins of antiquity, could claim of itself that "Not marble, nor the gilded monuments / Of princes, can outlive this powerful rhyme," so the world of fable could arise anew in a dense, complex, self-referential, and magnificently high-spirited poetry, rather than frozen into unenduring stone (the labyrinth was destroyed in 1775), and sounding only of the plashing of falling water, which is always nonsense until poetry makes it mean something.

Wandering through La Fontaine's world of fable is not in the least like going through one of the Sun King's labyrinths, but more like a walk through an English, or natural, sort of garden. The poet's muse, *"aux bords d'une onde pure,"* propounds its profusion of sorts of story, shades of ironic coloring, nuances of diction, turns of allegorizing strategy, and types of moral stance. But in all of these sorts of story it is what happens to them when they are *"mises en vers"* by this great poet that unifies them. The very verse itself—the so-called *vers libres* of rapidly shifting line-lengths and rhyming schemes (not to be confused with *vers libre,* the unrhymed "free verse" of Rimbaud and modernity)—creates a tone that could be unsatisfactorily characterized as "wry," "witty," "distanced"—all of which are true of it—but which does more than that. Both the zigzagging of the line lengths, and the unpredictabilities even of its mode of unpredictability (the very famous poem of the country rat and city rat is so regular in its quatrains of unvaryingly alternating lines of eight and seven syllables, cross-rhymed *abab,* that it is still sung as a children's song to a repeated melody), have both general and local effect. So, too, the wonderfully flexible diction, with its pointed and elegantly self-conscious use of archaic words here and there, and its constant reminders that *this* world of fable is like nobody else's. Even the American schoolchild who used to have to recite the line about the fox addressing the crow (and, of course, his cheese) in *à peu près ce langage* "in language [sort of? rather like? more or less? approximately?] like this" would get the *kind* of joke—in its self-reference to animal discourse, which is *à peu près langage, langue, parole* in any case, and to poetry, for which reality is always represented in *à peu près ce langage,* the language of the particular poem.

La Fontaine, the man who in daily life seems to have been devoted to truth-telling, avers that rhyming entails falsehood: *"Le mensonge et le vers de tout temps sont amis"*—"Lying and verse have always been friends." (Spector gives this normal alexandrine as a bumpy dactyllic pentameter, "Fiction and verse have always been friends through the ages" and Marianne Moore, "Of make-believe and verse, twined indivisibly," demonstrating an apparently inevitable drift toward embroidery, which sometimes, as here, merely falsifies, but in other instances, by other translators, can be rather like miming something in the original that remains silent in the translated language. But perhaps here is the point to consider questions other than those of what is usually called "accuracy".)

Two translations of the fables of La Fontaine into English verse have recently appeared, one of them complete, the other containing fifty selected ones, and they afford an excellent occasion for considering once again the ongoing questions of what is lost, or, possibly also found, in translation; of what verse translations can be variously *for,* in any case; and, of course, the greatness of La Fontaine's particular achievement. Perhaps also because of the celebrated failure of one of our major poets, Marianne Moore, to get *enough* right in her quirky, mannered versions (published without the French text *en face*) of all the *Fables choisies mises en vers* (Richard Howard's handful of versions in unrhymed syllabics do better with tone), the great seventeenth-century French poet's remarkable achievement continues to present an untamed challenge to poetic translation. *The Complete Fables of Jean de la Fontaine* by the late Professor Spector (he died in 1985) is a massive volume, with all the fables in both French and his freely accentual rhymed translations. For this, and for its completeness, we must be quite grateful. But it contains no apparatus whatsoever—no introduction, no explanatory or exploratory notes that might have further graced, and much further enhanced the utility of, this edition, and it is unfortunate that, the translator having died apparently before the project had been completed, some students or colleagues of his, consulting available materials, had not been able to provide what would certainly have been most useful to any reader needing and interested in having this corpus of poetry in English. Norman R. Shapiro's perfectly controlled iambic versions of *Fifty Fables of La Fontaine* have an introduction, and notes of some length, on nineteen of the poems.

The great early English printer William Caxton translated one of the many medieval collections from the French and published it in 1483. The fable with which La Fontaine opens book 1 of his great work appears thus in Caxton's early modern English (I have modernized the spelling and punctuation):

The xvii Fable is of the Ant and of the Cigale [grasshopper]. It is good to purvey himself in the summer season of such things whereof he shall myster [need] and have need in winter season, as thou mayst see by this present fable of the cigale, which in the winter time went and demanded of the ant some of her corn for to eat. And then the ant said to the cigale, "What hast thou done all the summer last passed?" And the cigale answered, "I have sung." And after said the ant to her, "Of my corn shalt thou none have. And if thou has sung all the summer, dance now in winter." And therefore there is one time for us to do some labor and work, and one time for to have rest. For he that worketh not nor doth no good shall have oft at his teeth great cold, and lack at his need.

It will be noticed that this little story has both what the Greeks called a *promythium* and an *epimythium* (or what we would call the "moral"), the *promythium* being originally a sort of indexing device whose function changed into that of introductory moral. La Fontaine's story of *La Cigale et la fourmi* is free of the explicit moralizing of either of these (although he uses both frequently in other fables) and we need go no further than its famous opening lines to see the quintessence of his art at work:

> La cigale, ayant chanté
>   Tout l'été
> Se trouva fort dépourvue
> Quand la bise fut venue:
> Pas un seul petit morceau
> De mouche ou de vermisseau . . .

[The cicada having sung / all summer / found herself quite destitute / when the winter wind came: / not a single tiny bit / of fly or worm . . .]

The normal promise of neoclassical verse to keep a metrical form going in a consistent pattern of line length and rhyming is sharply violated here, and to pointed effect: the summer of singing occurs in a radically shortened line, itself proleptic of the cutting-off of plenty by winter soon to be mentioned. It is not surprising to find both Shapiro and Spector translating the opening the same way—the strategy for responding to the effect seems inevitable:

The cricket having sung her song
All summer long
Found—when the winter wind blew free
Her cupboard bare as bare could be;
Nothing to greet her hungering eye;
No merest crumb of worm or fly.

(Shapiro)

Cicada having sung her song
All summer long,
Found herself without a crumb
When winter winds did come.
Not a scrap was there to find
Of fly or earthworm, any kind.

(Spector)

The *long/song* rhyme is indeed, apparently inevitable for mod-
ern translators: James Michie in his really fine versions of eighty-
two of the fables (1979; no French texts but a fine introduction
by Geoffrey Grigson), gives "The cicada, having chirped her
song / All summer long"; Francis Duke (1965; excellent appara-
tus of introduction; fascinating notes, and appendices) does it
"Locust, having sung her song / All summer long." Only
Moore's "Until fall a grasshopper / Chose to chirr," idiosyn-
cratic but not poetically *original,* departs from this, but her
"chirr" makes a blur of the sharp effect of the *long* in the short
line about the long summer. In Spector's version of the succeed-
ing lines two other problems arise that, I am sorry to say, mark
his translations throughout. All of the twenty lines of the poem
following the short one are in the same seven-syllable line, but
Spector varies "When winter winds did come" with six syllables
and three beats. Substituting differing patterns of line length for
La Fontaine's precise ones is often necessary, given the exigen-
cies of English stress and syntax; often the local effect of a short-
short-long pattern in three lines of the French, for example,
may be best handled by another pattern in the English. Yet in
this case, where the continued consistency is itself the mode, it
seems pointless. (Moore's metric in her versions is almost im-
penetrable, being neither consistently that of the strict syllabics
with half-audible rhyme of many of her own best poems, nor
normal iambic, nor indeterminate.) But the problem is that

Spector gives us the awkward "did come," which always reads in modern rhymed verse like archaizing filler, and although it might be argued that he was trying to catch the tense and aspect of *"fut venue,"* the effect is to weaken the movement of the line. This sort of thing happens continually in his English verse.

Shapiro never does this; there is always an assurance of metrical control, and a sharp aptness to his decisions about diction, so that when he makes an egregious emendation or substitution, it most often rings true. I prefer the somewhat startling adjustments he makes to the old familiar fable of the fox and the crow (even with the almost outrageous allusion at the very end) to something chaster but less neatly done. The sense of play in, and with, the translation is somehow an appropriate version of the poet's own:

> Perched on a treetop, Master Crow
>   Was clutching in his bill a cheese,
> When Master Fox, sniffing the fragrant breeze,
> Came by and, more or less, addressed him so:
>   "Good day to you, Your Ravenhood!
> How beautiful you are! How fine! How fair!
> Ah, truly, if your song could but compare
>   To all the rest, I'm sure you would
> Be dubbed the *rara avis* of the wood!"
> The crow, beside himself with joy and pride,
>   Begins to caw. He opens wide
>   His gawking beak; lets go the cheese; it
> Falls to the ground. The fox is there to seize it,
>   Saying: "You see? Be edified:
> Flatterers thrive on fools' credulity.
> The lesson's worth a cheese, don't you agree?"
>   The crow, shamefaced and flustered, swore—
>   Too late, however: "Nevermore!"

This may be perhaps the single fable most familiar to American readers, and to play with it requires some bravura. "Your Ravenhood" for good old *"Monsieur le Corbeau"* and *"Rara avis"* for *"le phénix des hôtes de ces bois"* are a little surprising, but by the time second thoughts have let them pass, they have already worked. More interesting to me is the sequence "His gawking beak; lets go the cheese; it / Falls to the ground. The fox is there to seize it," where the series of enjambed lines culminating in the half-stumbling "cheese; it" is followed across the line break by the falling of the cheese into another clause ending at the middle of a line. But the whole is elegantly saved, in a completed pentameter line, when the fox is there to seize not only the cheese but, we feel momentarily, the fragment of verse—the fox catching the cheese itself catches the falling half-line, in a move that is pleased with itself even as it gives pleasure.

Again, in the wonderful short fable of the mountain laboring to give birth to the ridiculous (in the proverb: *"et nascitur ridiculus mus"*) mouse, La Fontaine cannot resist moralizing it as a defense of his own retreat from epic inflation into the wisdom of shrewd minority. The pregnant mountain, shouting and screaming so that spectators are convinced she's about to give birth to a city huger than Paris, produces a mouse—in La Fontaine, everyone

> *Crut qu'elle accoucherait sans faute*
> *D'une cité plus grosse que Paris:*
> *Elle accoucha d'une Souris.*

Here the sublime rhyme of *Paris/Souris* almost does it all. There's no way to get that in English, even *house/mouse* missing the epic grandeur of the drop in scale. Shapiro doesn't try, and simply gives us "That all who run to watch surmise / She'll bear a city more than Paris' size. / A mouse is what she bore." He may indeed be playing off the bilingual *surmise/souris,* and taking some solace from that. Spector's

> A mountain straining in labor
> Uttered such a piercing cry
> That, rushing up, each neighbor
> Thought she'd deliver, up to the sky,
> A city greater than Paris therefore.
> A mouse is what she bore.

fails for me in many ways: the delivering "up to the sky" is so strained that it commits only the fault of parodic self-exemplification, the rhetoric straining to produce *"ridiculus mus."* Shapiro doesn't bemoan the loss of the Paris/mouse, and gets his (or, really, English's) own back at the end, when, after rendering beautifully the parody of epic opening in La Fontaine, he catches better than any other translator the magnificent deflation at the end. La Fontaine avers that

> *Quand je songe à cette fable*
> *Dont le récit est mentaur*
> *Et le sense et véritable,*
> *Je me figure un auteur*
> *Qui dit: "Je chanterai la guerre*
> *Qui firent les Titans au maître du tonnerre."*
> *C'est promettre beaucoup: mais qu'en sort-il souvent?*
> *Du vent.*

This final tiniest line, with its full rhyme, reminds us once again how "hot air" (in its rhetorical sense) has density of matter inverse to its expansiveness, like bad pseudopoetic rhetoric. Here Shapiro is immensely satisfying:

> When I conceive this fiction
> Empty of fact but full of sense,
> It seems to me a true depiction
> Of authors' vain grandiloquence.
> They promise: "Ah, my lyre will sing
> Of Titans' combat with the Thunder's king."
> Fine words! And yet what comes to pass?
> Just gas.

His additions all come from so deep a grasp of the matter that at worst, they spell out and gloss the issues (e.g., the "vain grandiloquence" and the "my lyre will sing" as an English neoclassic cliché to parallel *"Je chanterai"*). It may also be noticed that Spector will very often translate an alexandrine in the French by some kind of accentual long line in the English, as here:

> "I'll now sing of that war
> That Titans waged, to the master of thunder's door."
> That's promising a lot, but what often comes out of there?
> Hot air.

Shapiro, as in his version of these lines, seems almost to feel viscerally the way in which the English pentameter always stands in for the alexandrine—it's the same "official," canonical line—

and he uses it in this passage, as elsewhere, appropriately. But in general, it is his ear for English iambic verse that is so well tuned that his lines have the sort of authority of their own that gives credence to his strategies of adaptation and adumbration. His diction, also, seems remarkably flexible in exactly the right way.

I would particularly commend the ending of "The Dog Who Drops His Prey for Its Reflection," and the serious high mode of the closing of the fable of "The Oak and the Reed," the story of how it's better, when the heavy storm comes, to be able to bend so as not to have to break—a fable inevitably political. La Fontaine tells of the uprooting of *"Celui de qui la tête au ciel étoit voisine / Et dont les peids touchoient à l'empire des morts,"* which Shapiro catches up in the wind's uprooting "the one, who, just before, / Had risen heavenward with lofty head, / Whose feet had reached the empire of the dead." Spector's "The tree whose top thrust upward to heaven's domain, / And whose roots reached down toward the realm of the dead" is to be faulted not for its free-accentual looseness, but for the lack of point and effectiveness in its deployment, here as throughout.

In other instances, this causes his version to lose the point of proverbial lines so famous in the French tradition that it's hard to know whether the poet has coined, or is merely quoting them, for example, the opening of the fable of the wolf and the lamb, which begins *"La raison du plu fort est toujours le meilleure; / Nous l'allons montrer tout à l'heure,"* which Spector gives as "The strong are always best at proving they're right. / Witness the case we're now going to cite." But Shapiro's "The strongest argue best, and always win. / Read on: you'll find the proof thereof herein," although it pads the second line a little and defers the *"tout à l'heure,"* makes up for it with the touch of wit in "thereof herein," and certainly gives the opening line its due. (If liberties are to be taken with it, I much prefer the artful chiasm of Elizur Wright [1841]: "The strongest reasons always yield / To reasons of the strongest." On the other hand, an earlier English translator who takes unpardonable liberties that often totally deflect the moral point, Robert Thomson, represents the excesses of syntatic inversion in "Strength upon right with ease can trample, / As will appear by this example.")

The one advantage of Spector's version is its completeness, and with the accompanying French text it can be of use for reference, which makes the lack of any annotation even more unfortunate. (Even a line or two about each fable's source, which could have been added even from Fournier's 1839 edition, let alone fuller glosses from the fuller edition of Regnier almost fifty years later, would have been welcome.) It is indeed too bad that Shapiro did not give us some of the celebrated longer pieces, such as the moral essay addressed to Madame de la Sablière that concludes book 9, or the wonderful *Les Compagnons d'Ulysse,* in which the poet, following Plutarch and other writers, works a splendid turn on Circe's magic. Ulysses' men, each transformed into a different sort of beast, all elect, with powerful pragmatic and satiric arguments, to remain animals rather than be returned to human form: *"Ils croyaient s'affranchir suivants leurs passions, / Ils étaient esclaves d'eux-mêmes"* (Spector: "They thought indulging their passions had set them free; / Slaves of themselves, it would seem"; but even with its late-romantic syntactic inversion, Elizur Wright is tighter, and avoids the weak passing move of "it would seem," there for the rhyme: "Where passion led, they thought their course was free; / Self-bound their chains they could not see." Here again, Spector has no ear for epigrammatic closure, and I long to hear what Shapiro would do with this). And I also miss, in the handsomely designed and produced Shapiro volume, the analogous bite and deft turning of Grandville's celebrated illustrations, rather than the bland ones that are included: the jacket blurb suggests that they may have been chosen as being appropriate for children, but that would make the way in which they merely depict literal animals, instead of allegories, even less helpful. Shapiro's version reads aloud wonderfully, whether for children or adults, and works for readers with or without knowledge of the originals. In fact, the better you know them, the more pleasure his translations can give.

Among the fables Shapiro does include are two of the kind that would not be thought of by most readers as Aesopian. One, the fable of Discord mentioned earlier, continues her story from Olympian surroundings to subsequent human life, by giving her a father named "Thine-and-Mine," and a brother, "True-False," and having her end up in residence in the inn of marriage. The other is an etiological fable of the blinding of Cupid (a favorite Renaissance motif, investigated over fifty years ago by Erwin Panofsky, pointed up by the fine ambiguity of the phrase "Love is blind": it could mean that Cupid, blindfolded, shoots his arrows randomly, as well as that all lovers are blind to truths about their desires' objects and themselves as well), *L'Amour et la folie*. The translator's skill and wit come through beautifully in it, and I can make no better recommendation of his work in closing than by quoting the entire narrative part, starting with its fine handling of the internal rhyme in the original's *"La Folie et l'Amour jouoient un jour ensemble"*:

> Folly and Love, one day at play together,
> Had a dispute. The latter wondered whether
> The Council of the Gods ought not be called.
>   Folly, incensed, punched, flailed away
> And robbed the other of the light of day;
> Whose mother, Venus, properly appalled—
> Shrieking for vengeance, woman that she was—
> Deafened the gods and won them to her cause:
>   Nemesis, Jove, Hell's judges too—
>   In short, the whole Olympian crew.
> "No punishment is hard enough," she pleaded;
>   "My son is now an invalid.
> Do what you have to do!" The court acceded,
>   And so, indeed, do it they did:
> In view of public weal and private woe,
> They sentenced Folly evermore to go
> Abroad with Love, withersoever,
> And be his constant guide, forever.

Quadrophenia
Translating the Pessoas

If Fernando Pessoa had never existed, Jorge Luis Borges might have had to invent him. This remarkable modern poet started writing in English, in which he was educated; and then, in his native Portuguese, he produced four major poetic oeuvres, one under his own name and three completely different ones by fictional poets—no mere pseudonyms—called Alberto Caeiro, Álvaro de Campos, and Ricardo Reis. This was not a matter of tragic, literal psychiatric disorder; it was a figurative revision of a multiple poetic personality that, with its complex relations among the "heteronyms" (as they are usually called to distinguish them from mere pseudonyms without full fictional identities for their bearers), betokened a strong, original, and stable poetic imagination confronting some of the major problems of modernism.

A consideration of Pessoa's poetry entails knowledge of the work of all four poets. Professional scholars will also be concerned with a number of Pessoa's other, more shadowy heteronymous figures: the authors of some of the early poems in English, Alexander Search and Charles Robert Anon; and, in Portuguese, C. Pacheco and a critic named Bernard Soares who wrote no verse, and a number of others to a projected total of nineteen. But it is ultimately the trilogy of poets Caeiro, Campos, and Reis—along with the orthonymic poetry, written fully in propria persona, of Pessoa himself—that is of primary importance.

Pessoa was born in Lisbon in 1888, the descendant, on his father's side, of a Jewish convert to Christianity (hence, perhaps,

Review-essay of Fernando Pessoa, *New Republic,* September 7, 1987.

the Jewish element in Campos's character). Pessoa's father was a music critic who died when the boy was five. His mother then married the Portuguese consul in Durban, and Pessoa was educated in South Africa, leaving it permanently in 1905 after having written a prize essay for admission to university there. He chose to attend the University of Lisbon, and in that city he remained, from 1908 until his death in 1935. He worked at commercial foreign correspondence for a number of firms in Lisbon, led a literary life that touched avant-garde circles, and published poems, translations, and essays. He never married, but lived both alone and with members of his family.

Until 1909 Pessoa wrote in English; there are over one hundred English poems. (A responsible edition of all of Pessoa's English writings should be done.) Three years later he began to write in his native language and to read widely in French Symbolist poetry. By 1915 he was writing poems under all three heteronyms, at first publishing only some under the name of Campos.

In a letter dated ten months before his death, Pessoa told a disciple his story of the genesis of the heteronyms: suddenly, on March 8, 1914, he started writing a large number of poems under the covering title *O Guardador de Rebanhos* (*The Keeper of Sheep*)—perhaps, it has been suggested, transforming an earlier abandoned project of inventing, as a hoax, a strange sort of pastoral poet. But Alberto Caeiro is a very belated pastoralist. "I never kept sheep," begins the first of the forty-nine poems that make up his collected works, "But it's as if I'd done so." Here is the rest of the first strophe of his proem, in Edwin Honig and Susan M. Brown's excellent new translation:

> My soul is like a shepherd.
> It knows wind and sun
> Walking hand in hand with the Seasons
> Observing, and following along.
> All of Nature's unpeopled peacefulness
> Comes to sit alongside me.
> Still I'm sad, as a sunset is
> To the imagination,
> When it grows cold at the end of the plain
> And you feel the night come in
> Like a butterfly through the window.

The plain but quizzical style, the limpid vers libre, the systematic dramaturgy—all give Caeiro's work a power that is never simplistic.

The other heteronyms emerged around Caeiro. According to Pessoa's letter, Caeiro was born in 1889, lived with an old aunt in the country, was only minimally educated, had no profession, and died at twenty-six; he represents, for Pessoa, what Shelley called "unpremeditated art." Ricardo Reis, a Horatian neoclassicist in whose tight, strophic odes meditation seems to crystallize, was born in 1887, says Pessoa, and was educated by the Jesuits; a doctor, he resided in Brazil because of his monarchist views. Álvaro de Campos, a naval engineer not presently employed, lives in Lisbon; he is well traveled, the author (like Reis and Pessoa) of critical writings, as well as of Whitmanesque longish rhapsodic poems in a mode of free verse very different from Caeiro's.

And finally, of course, there is the orthonymic Fernando Pessoa. The rhymed lyrics of his *Cancioneiro,* and of the wonderful long sequence published in 1934 called *Mensagem* ("message," "dispatch"—the word can also be used to mean "errand" or "summons") seem to connect the different virtues of Campos and Reis. *Mensagem* is a sort of post-Symbolist revision of Vaz de Camões's *Os Lusiadas,* the great Portuguese Renaissance epic, a series of internalized, meditative lyrics on moments and figures in Portuguese history, perhaps in some ways analogous to Hart Crane's *The Bridge.*

What is most Borgesian—or possibly Nabokovian—about this group of poets is the way in which Pessoa himself acknowledges how deep an influence Caeiro was upon his own work: "Alberto Caeiro is my master." Octavio Paz has commented that "Caeiro is the sun in whose orbit Reis, Campos, and Pessoa himself rotate. In each are particles of negation or unreality. Reis believes in form, Campos in sensation, Pessoa in symbols. Caeiro doesn't believe in anything. He exists." And Pessoa remarked of Caeiro's influential force:

> Caeiro had that force. What does it matter to me that Caeiro be of me if Caeiro is like that? So, operating on Reis, who had not as yet written anything, he made come to birth in him a form of his

own and an aesthetic persona. So operating on myself, he has delivered me from shadows and letters. . . . After this, so prodigiously achieved, who will ask whether Caeiro exists or not?

There are other ways of regarding this relation among the four poets, three of whom have been invented by a fourth who nonetheless claims to derive from one of them. Pessoa invoked at various times the analogy of fully formed Shakespearean characters, and at others the context of modernist poetic impersonality. As Álvaro de Campos put it, in a manifesto called *Ultimatum,* the greatest artist will reveal himself the least (this from a true, not a trivial, Whitmanian). He will "write in the greatest number of literary genres, making use of paradoxes and dissimilarities. No artist should have only one personality."

A poet like Auden, who wrote in a variety of modes, could approximate this achievement, although his voice never changes. So can a dramatic monologuist, of which Pessoa might seem to be an extreme case. But there is another aspect to his Trilogy: it is as if the historical phases of the life of poetry itself, not merely of one artist's work, were being personified synchronically and allowed to coexist. What Renaissance scholars refer to as the Virgilian progression—from pastoral to georgic to epic—was affirmed in the canceled opening lines of the *Aeneid,* which outlined, for Renaissance poets, the model of a poetic career: "I am he who once played my song on a slender reed, then, leaving the woods, made the neighboring fields serve the farmer, however grasping—a book farmers prize; but now of Mars' bristling [arms and the man I sing . . .]."

Similarly, Caeiro's modern pastoral, the Parnassian withdrawals of Reis, Campos's great odes of imagined voyaging, are all gathered up in various ways in Pessoa's own poems. Certainly the *Mensagem* would not be possible without Caeiro's unmediated vision, or Reis's forethought, or Campos's unending quest for a hero, a subject, at once within and beyond himself. The various heteronyms can thus be heard as giving voice to drifts, strains, and impulses within one imagination, each providing a reductive version of what the revisionary New Poetry should be.

There have been several books introducing Pessoa to speakers of English, but they are all out of print. Aside from Edouard

Roditi's brief essay and fine, pioneering translations of five poems in 1955, we have had a Penguin volume by Jonathan Griffin and two very useful books, both published in 1971 and both with detailed introductions and notes—one of sixty poems, translated by F. E. G. Quintanilha, and the other by Peter Rickard of Cambridge, an exemplary volume of seventy poems with excellent apparatus and free-verse translations of unusual tautness and limpidity. Both of these include the Portuguese texts, and for readers without that language but with, say, French and Spanish, the originals can be a revelation: with a dictionary, an elementary grammar, and a good knowledge of poetry, one can find out a great deal about what has been traded for what in the complex economy of verse translation.

Now Edwin Honig, who produced a smaller selection of Pessoa translations in 1971, has collaborated with Susan M. Brown on two volumes. One is a broader selection of the work of all the heteronyms, as well as of Pessoa's own English verse. The other is the complete version of Caeiro's *The Keeper of Sheep*. Honig and Brown are at their best with Caeiro, and the complete oeuvre is a treasure to have. I regret strongly that there is no facing Portuguese text, particularly in the more comprehensive selection, *Poems of Ferdinand Pessoa*. Without the Portuguese, and without the kind of biographical material and annotation that Rickard gives, the poems of Reis and of Pessoa himself lose the most. Explaining some of the problems faced by the translations in Honig and Brown's larger volume involves taking a closer look at all the poets and their work. (When quoting from poems that Honig and Brown do not translate, I use my own provisional versions.)

We might start with Pessoa's poems in English. They are worth more than a glance, not least because some of their peculiar energies and successes carry over into the later work and are immediately accessible to English readers. The series of "Inscriptions," resonant of the sepulchral epigrams of the Greek Anthology, seems related to the mode of Ricardo Reis. They are terse, elegant, graceful, and yet capable of startling:

> Me, Chloe, a maid, the mighty fates have given,
> Who was nought to them, to the peopled shades.

Thus the gods will. My years were but twice seven.
I am forgotten now in my distant glades.

Or:

There was a silence where the town was old.
Grass grows where not a memory lies below.
We that dined loud are sand. The tale is told.
The far hoofs hush. The inn's last light doth go.

Or:

I put by pleasure like an alien bowl.
Stern, separate, mine, I looked towards where gods seem.
From behind me the common shadow stole.
Dreaming that I slept not, I slept my dream.

"My hand / Put these inscriptions here, half knowing why; / Last, and hence seeing all, of the passing band," concludes the fictional author in the last of these, as if Pessoa were bidding farewell, in 1920, to neoclassicism, summing up and transcending a tradition in a way analogous to that by which Alberto Caeiro would perform a final revision of pastoral.

Honig and Brown reprint ten of Pessoa's strange, somewhat crabbed English sonnets and some earlier poems, including a few by Alexander Search. One misses a bit of the long, homosexually-oriented "Antinous" (1915) that begins (with an echo of Verlaine, I think), "The rain outside was cold in Hadrian's soul," and whose high diction moves through fine passages like this one about Hadrian's eponymous lover:

That love they lived as a religion
Offered to gods that come themselves to men.
Sometimes he was adorned or made to don
Half-vestured, then in statued nudity
Did imitate some god that seems to be
By marble's accurate virtue men's again.

And the remarkable heterosexual counterpart of the Antinous poem, Pessoa's "Epithalamium" of the previous year (a weird version of Spenser, deriving from his diction and verse-form but without the famous refrain), concentrates on the fears and joys of the bride's sexual initiation. Thus the twelfth strophe's invocation of a phallic "belfry's height" that "Does in the blue wide heaven a message prove, / Somewhat calm, of delight," and of the sun pouring light on the "ordered rout" of guests; "And all their following eyes clasp round the bride":

> They feel like hands her bosom and her side;
> Like the inside of her vestment next her skin,
> They round her round and fold each crevice in;
> They lift her skirts up, as to tease or woo
> The cleft thing hid below. . . .

The verbal texture and formal control of the English poems operate with greater density and plangency in Pessoa's own poems and, differently, in those of Reis. What marks Caeiro, though, is that he is always telling you what he is *not* doing: "Rhymes don't matter to me," he says. "You seldom see / Two identical trees, standing side by side." Still, he can be allusive in his negations of allusiveness and tradition, as in his rejection of the mainstream of poetic history in favor of the river flowing through his own village. (One's local stream was the emblem of one's own poetic turf throughout the Renaissance, like the Thames, the Avon, Du Bellay's Loire, and so on.) But he ends poem 20 by saying that his village river reminds one of nothing, that if one is beside it one is merely beside it. The passing wind, in another poem, talks only about the wind; the Virgilian shepherds, in yet another, played on reeds and sang in a literary way about love, "But the shepherds in Virgil poor things / are Virgil, / And nature is ancient and beautiful." He keeps protesting his conceptual innocence and performing, like Wallace Stevens's snow man, a reduction of false imaginings.

Álvaro de Campos is a visionary wanderer, most obviously indebted for his ode forms and long rhapsodic lines to Whitman; but he is also a Shelleyan. His early "Triumphal Ode" (1914), tinged with Futurist rhetoric, starts out

> In the aching light of the factory's large electric bulbs,
> Fevered, I write.
> I write gnashing my teeth, brutal before the beauty of this,
> Before the beauty of this, wholly unknown to the ancients. . . .

> Fevered and staring at the engines as if at a tropical Nature
> Great human tropics of iron and fire and power—
> I sing, and sing the present, and also the past and future.
> Because the present is all of the present and all of the future
> And Plato and Virgil within the machines and electric lights.

But, after much Whitmanesque incantation, this poem ends with a longing for transcendence, and a revision of Whitman's favored trope: *"Ah nõ ser en toda a gente e toda a parte!"* ("Ah not to be all people and all places!").

Campos's long, splendid "Maritime Ode," with its sexual fantasies and Mallarméan withdrawals and fears of erotic shipwreck, his "Tobacco-shop," his poems on "Lisbon Revisited," move into realms of terror, despair, and self-questioning of a sort Caeiro's pure assurance never explores. His diction, too, wanders from high to low. It seems to me, with my limited knowledge of Portuguese that Honig and Brown do very well with his language and with the cadence of his lines.

Ricardo Reis is another story. He invokes Horace's Lydias, Naearas, and Chloes, without any of Caeiro's desire to avoid singing literarily of love:

> As though every kiss
> Were of departure
> O my Chloe, let us kiss now, loving.
> Perhaps this hand touching
> Our shoulders already
> Hails that barge, empty ever when it comes,
> Binding in the same sheaf
> What we were together
> With the totality of other life.

In highly crafted, syllabically counted lines, and with archaized diction and Latinate syntax, Reis promotes a guarded, intellectual, far-from-ecstatic mood of carpe diem and memento mori intertwined, asking nothing of the gods, the answer to life's questions lying beyond them: *"Os deus sõ deuses / Porque nõ se pensam"* ["The gods are gods / Because they don't think themselves up"]. Literally echoing Horace, Reis proclaims that "Happy he whom gracious life / Allowed to keep the gods in mind / To see like them / These earthly things where dwells / A reflection, mortal, of immortal life." Where Caeiro rejects previous allegorizations of nature, Reis rejects moral homilies on our condition, except that he propounds the virtue of such rejections:

> To everyone, like his height justice is
>   Distributed: thus fate makes
>   Some tall and others happy.
> Nothing is a prize: what happens just happens.
>   Nothing, Lydia, do we
>   Owe our fate but to have it.

To preserve in English something of the tone of Reis's syntax and diction (he will use Latin words that are neologisms for modern Portuguese) and his meter (it substitutes for the classical quantitative prosody a pure syllabism) is not too difficult, and syllabic versions of Reis would give one a better sense of the almost classically modernist (in the Anglo-American, rather than the Continental mode) use of strict form as a stay against confusion. In a central, aristocratic figure, Reis rises above the storms of sensibility through which Campos perilously and ecstatically navigates: "Be whole in everything. Put all you are / Into the smallest thing you do. / The whole moon gleams in every pool, / It rides so high." (Thus Honig and Brown, although the *"a lu a toda / Brilha, porque alta vive"* given as the full moon "riding high"—rather than dwelling at such heights— also appears in Roditi.) Any attempt to get at Reis's syntax can run aground, though. In the lovely poem beginning *"As rosas amo dos jardins de Adonis / Essas volucres, amo, Lidia, rosas, / Que em o dia em que nasem, / Ém esse dia morem"* ["The roses I love of the Gardens of Adonis, those transitory I love, Lydia, roses that on the day they are born, on that day they die"] something of the Latinate word-order may be easier to get than the *volucres* (not a Portuguese word, but a Latin one meaning "winged" and used by Horace to mean "fleeting"). Honig and Brown give us a wrenching and awkward shift to start with:

> I the roses love in the garden of Adonis,
> Lydia, I love those fast fleeting roses
>   That on the same day they are born
>   On that same day they die.

I much prefer Edouard Roditi's 1955 version, which, with its emphasis on the Latin sense of "fugitive" (for *volucres)* resonates with an analogous English neoclassicism.

Reis has not yet had his optimum translator. Perhaps, as is frequently the case with poetic translation, a poem in Language A must pass into Language B through the enabling filter of some particular body of poetry already in B. (Recall, for example, the Tennyson that makes the blank verse of Robert Fitzgerald's wonderful English *Aeneid* so noble and powerful, as opposed to the tincture of Pound that made the same translator's *Odyssey* so strong for the modernist ear.) Perhaps the youthful Milton's unrhymed, stressed translation of Horace, "What slender youth . . . ," might provide something of such a filter. Or so might some of the diction of Landor.

The so-called orthonymic poetry of Pessoa himself requires even more in the way of adaptive resources. Pessoa has all of the control of Reis with none of his archaisms, and he has also a good deal of Campos's vigor. His negations and withdrawals are almost gnostic in their complexity and go beyond Caeiro in wiping the slate clean. Thus in a Christmas poem of 1922 (the original rhymes, as in this version, are the words *culto* and *occulto*):

> A god is born. Others die. What never came
> Nor went was Truth. Error changed all the more.
> Our new Eternity is not the same.
> The best is always what has gone before.
> Blind, Knowledge labors at the barren ground.
> Crazy, Faith lives the dream of its own cult.
> A newborn god is just a new word's sound.
> Seek not then, nor believe. All is occult.

Pessoa's own verse makes rich and powerful use of rhyme, not merely for generating a melody or for pacing, but (as with all important poets) for its semantic work and play, for what it reveals of relations among words and among their referents— relations that ordinary usage keeps hidden. A poem of 1913 about a village church bell, for example, concludes:

> At each one of your strokes
> Resounding in open sky

I feel the past more distant
I feel longing more nigh

—except that in the original, the rhymes are on *aberto* ("open")
and *mais perto* ("nearer"): the widening of possibility becomes
another kind of enclosure at the incursion of *saudade* ("long-
ing," "yearning").

In another quatrain of the same poem, Pessoa plays with the
notion of repetition, saying of his village bell, sad in the evening
calm, "Each stroke of yours / Sounds within my soul"—bland
enough in English, except that the third line about each stroke
of the bell, *"Cada sua badalada,"* plays on the internal rhyme of
cada ("every") and the word for the tolling of a bell, as if thereby
to augment the number of strokes of the clapper.

One more example—they blossom everywhere in these
poems—of Pessoa's verbal texture, which gets completely lost in
most translations I've seen. "The Portuguese Sea," poem 30 of
Mensagem, ends:

> *Quem quer passar além da Bojador*
> *Tem que passar além da dor*
> *Deus ao mar o perigo e o abismo deu*
> *Mas nele é que espelhou a céu.*

In Honig and Brown:

> If you'd sail beyond the cape
> Sail you must past cares, past grief.
> God gave perils to the sea and sheer depth
> But mirrored heaven there.

But even without knowing any Portuguese, a reader can see the
symmetry of sailing past the *Bojador* (a West African promontory,
slightly south of the Canaries, once a limit of exploration) and
the *dor,* the anguish now seen as its last port, in the rhymed
shorter line. The pun that mirrors *Deus* and *deu,* "God" and
"gave," at the end of the next line is itself brilliantly avowed in the
final one, with its image of mirroring and the confirming rhyme
of *céu*—"sky," "heaven." One can't ask a translator to get all of
these moments, but one does keep wanting to be reminded that

they, or something like them, are there, that the language of the poetry has that sort of dimension.

If English syllabics suggest a way of handling Reis's tight strophes, perhaps a way of handling Pessoa's orthonymic poetry has been pointed by Richard Howard in the superb unrhymed but accentual-syllabic verse he used for all of Baudelaire. Howard managed, in versions of poems with rhyming stanzas just like Pessoa's, to create the impression of rhyme by his end-stopping mono- and disyllabic words; one has the feeling that the line one had just read had rhymed with an earlier one, heard but forgotten. Rhythm is more important than rhyme for holding verse together, even though it cannot often perform the magic on particular words that rhyme, assonance, and alliteration can.

Honig and Brown have done very well by Caeiro, and reasonably well by Álvaro de Campos. Ricardo Reis and Pessoa himself still may have to find their translators. But if Honig and Brown's work renews the debate about translation and leads to new versions of Pessoa, that, too, will be a measure of its success. Meanwhile this volume has brought a great poet to our attention again. Anybody who cares about poetry, about fictions of identity, about the whole of modernism, must be grateful.

III

Some Other Poets

Fabulous Traveler

Daryl Hine

Daryl Hine's beautiful and powerful volume called Daylight Saving opens on the wintry light of a January morning, in a group of aphorisms touching on late beginnings, cold, unpromising dawns, and metaphors of origination, but all full of a rueful gratitude for what that light, thin and cold, "precious" and "eleemosynary," can yet give. But that light has a particular tinge to it: at the end of "The Copper Beech" from *Minutes* of more than ten years earlier, Hine invokes the tree—"Whose shade is not the green of contemplation / But the imagination's rich metallic colour / Wherein, under libido, we live"—eroticizing the light and air of the end of Stevens's "Esthétique du Mal" and invoking the unstated words *believe, love,* and *leave,* which share an Indo-European base with "libido," and help it reach out toward the etymologically unrelated "live." If for minor writers wordplay is an evasion of depth, a mere rippling of surface, for a true poet it is not, perhaps because words are more than merely coins or counters for him. For Hine, words are bodies, not so much in the way Milton reminded himself in *Areopagitica* that texts are more like people than like things, but in the ways by which they can embrace or hurt or overpower or protect each other. Poems that are ordinarily tropes for acts of love become even more than that—the scene of a figure of love at another level. This is one of the reasons why Daryl Hine's prodigious wit, classical learning, and formal control never work like neometaphysical, or *libertin,* or even scholastic conceptual machinery to grind up passion into the stuff of joke. His devices, routines of moralization of landscape and meditative emblem-reading, his

---

In part from *Canto* 3 (1979); in part from *Yale Review* 73 (fall 1983).

mythographies and reinterpretations of themes and topoi that seem to flourish wherever he walks and turns his poetic eyes— all of these point beyond themselves and beyond, even, the points they purport to make.

For his control of learning and wit I can think of few poets alive that can approach him—the contractions of J. V. Cunningham, the exuberance of A. D. Hope are distant kin—and absolutely nobody of his age. Hine's access to a range of vocabularies is remarkable, and is always executed with a gentle ease, a *sprezzatura* marked by generosity rather than scorn. Thus, for example, this stanza from "Blight on Elm":

> Remember how we used to watch them change
> Their drip-dry garments spring and fall
> From green to brown and back again.
> This is how the suburbs lose their cool.
> By a coincidence never really strange
> The end in view is nearly natural,
> The beautiful laid level with the plain.

The punning between usage levels ("drip-dry" and "lose their cool"), the play with *plain* and *fancy* and *plane,* the radical revisionary enjambments that give discovered revised readings to "change" (intransitive becoming transitive) and "fall" (noun to verb)—to point these out is merely to identify the speaker's dialect. This is not poetry merely because of their presence. That mere presence makes such a passage splendid writing; but it is made poetry by what that writing is for and about: the parable of our very reading and comprehension of the effects. For instance, in these lines, the perception of a relation between catastrophe and its role in a natural cycle (possibly redemptive thereby, possibly not) is like a perception of enjambment. So, too, with the Tocquevilleian overtones of the leveling of beauty in democracy. The woods have continued to decay and fall from Virgil on, but unless there continues to be a renewal of signification in glimpses of the event, the observation is only worthy of the nature column in the newspaper.

Again, in "Codex," Hine's meditation on his own notebook page reaches back in order to go truly forward. The rueful precision of his characterization of diary notations as "Private convictions on parole" makes a significant and parabolic use of the punned-upon relation between words and a given word (as upon beliefs and sentences, both declarative and for terms in jail). But the poem also points back to the important invention, in late classical times, of the codex, or paged book, to supplant the roll. For Hine, the notebook is newly discovered in its opportunities for revisions and closures; the additional pun on coding provides those connections between the inscriptions of text and the enciphered messages of the rest of life. Thus the final stanza can complete, and close off, the meditation with another of those colloquial-traditional punning moves, provided by a found correspondence that itself makes the wordplay moot:

> Distillation of a thought
> Secreted in the honeycomb
> Whose flowery images succumb
> To hyperbole, dry rot,
> Preserved upon the notebook page,
> A catchword and a calendar
> A habit and a hermitage . . .
> Close it like a closet door.

In truth the prison of book unto which we doom ourselves sometimes a prison is, and Hine's little misprision of that imprisonment cuts close to some of the most sophisticated points now being made by theorists of text about such questions.

I have chosen some of the less startling passages from *Daylight Saving* to show how even in aphoristic moments, ultimate questions of the highest seriousness are being raised. It is also the case that they exemplify Hine's brilliant vernacular, always in the employ of his questing attention. The poet as traveler has always been central in his work; as early as in the prodigiously promising *The Devil's Picture Book*, published when Hine was twenty-three, he had observed how Circe "shapes the moral traveller," and since then, as voyager and voyeur, he has traveled the literal globe and the trophed sphere of language.

But this traveler is not Elizabeth Bishop's north-south voyager, and vastly different from the time traveler in Merrill, or Ashbery's metaphysical sidewalker. What he encounters and discovers, the places and scenes and ruins and visions he visits, the thoroughfares and byways he takes, the ways in which he loses his way—all of these occur in and about the mirrored world of language as well. The poet's voyeuristic gaze is as much riveted upon the verbal copulars as upon the mere physical instances of them. His own private revision of "Le Monocle de Mon Oncle" in another poem of love at near-forty ("My Optics") makes an itinerary of his relation to his own eyeglasses, which culminates in one of those remarkable, inevitably self-referential, moments of self-portraiture:

> Often in the act of
> Sex they are abandoned.
> Balanced at the bedside
> See our twin prescriptions
> Gleam, a pair of glasses
> Disaffected, empty,
> Drained of speculation.
> Touchingly myopic,
> Lovers, twenty, forty,
> Put their faith in contacts.
> (Parenthetically
> Feeling is believing.)

The imagination sees truly with the eyes' glasses off, and even the convex and concave parentheses (including the virtual ones, given the effect of the enjambment, around the word "parenthetically" itself) help to focus the mind's attention, allowing it to recognize the occasional intimacy of its otherwise distant handmaid, the sense of touch. That is why the revision of "seeing is believing" is not an empty joke. That is why the pun on the recently colloquial "contacts" for "contact lenses" is not only appropriate, but self-glossing. For the average contemporary poet like Wallace Stevens's who does not make the visible a little hard to see, diction is a matter of style, and at most of tone. It is either that the low and colloquial are sincere, direct, casual, bare, and authentic—or that they can be ruefully employed by the belated Poundian mentality to remind us how far things have fallen, how deeply the dialect of the tribe has been corrupted. But for the true poet, learned in the biology of language, the life of words is a figure for the life of human beings, and the dialectic of early and late uses is too serious a business to be reduced to the uses of mockery, of siding with the kids or the old people. For most writers of verse, this brutal and ridiculous "cloven fiction," as Blake called it, produces the stylistic factions of New and Old, Now and Then, and manifests itself as the groupies versus Lawrence Welk. The true poet is chained to the drivel of this sort of distinction by the sad necessities of literary kinship. But he or she will have no part of it; and Hine's mode of moving between the learned and the ordinary meanings of words is one of his principal means of transportation.

In the wonderful suite-poem, "Arrondissements," Hermes and Apollo accompany the wanderer through a Paris that lies both in and far beyond Baedeker's; like the brilliant "Vowel Movements" of his previous volume, *Resident Alien,* and the more overtly paradigmatic, alphabetically arrayed "Linear A" in that same book, this district-by-district itinerary opens with what is, in its local way, a statement of poetic theory:

> A foreign city in a foreign language:
> Errors you will find your way around
> Less by misconstruction of an image
> Idiomatic as the underground
> Than by reference to the lost and found
> Out-of-date semantic luggage
> And archaic sentimental slang which
> Used to mean so much. Beware of the sound,
> Volumes of experience rebound,
> Sense can take care of itself.

This mapping of place onto word is underlined and demonstrated by such rubrics as the miniature independent plot to the rhymes—the kind that the late W. K. Wimsatt taught readers to observe—that moves from *language* to *image* to *luggage* to *slang which* (and thereby, *"slanguage"*), and will end, in the rest of the stanza, in *baggage, dommage,* and *youth from age* (the poem instructs a younger companion). At one moment of waking, in the VIème, the traveler observes how "Again today deciphers pornographic / Night's incomprehensible design, / Every superstitious hieroglyphic / Reified by an explicit sun" and we are reminded again of the sentimental nature of all of the poet's journeying.

For in the world of this novelist, travel writer, and preeminently electrifying poet, Eros is in every place, in every topic.

Like the graffiti that the errant eye of the speaker in these poems everywhere encounters, the signature of sex is inscribed on almost every available surface, even on the walls of words and phrases—which for the unalienated resident, or the linguistic stay-at-home, remain otherwise blank. But it is only the nonreader who is put off—or, in fact, on—by them: in such poems as "Atlantic and Pacific," "Amor es Sueño," "Free Love," and others, the manifest erotic meditation holds a torch up to the surrounding world. In emblematic investigations of a constellation ("Coma Berenices") and the TV screen ("Prime Time") the quest for significance—that primary modern metaphor of erotic questing—diverts the wanderer who is nonetheless impelled by the same motion. In his beautiful sonnet to the great seventeenth-century Spaniard, Luis de Góngora, a distant precursor, Hine maps his travels in the realms of silver. The two initial lines, the reader may notice, conclude with the only two rhyme-words in the poem, and they embrace the major metaphor of language and world through which, and with which, this remarkable conquistador moves. The poem deserves quotation entire:

> To your language if not your native land,
> Which is a tongue when all is said
> That's done, perverse, gold, standard, and
> Curiously conservative, as dead
> As anything Amerigo invented,
> I pilgrim with my accents in my hand
> And your conceits unequalled in my head
> Through volumes of rock and canticles of sand.
> Like paradise, you are a promised land
> Aflow with ilk and money, brine and wed-
> lock, secrets that like circumstances stand
> Unalterable, maps to be misread.
> Were we translated here and now, instead
> Of reading we might understand.

Hine's virtuosity is such that it knows where to leave off, as well as where to overwhelm. A rather important poem in *Daylight Saving* (relevant to his whole oeuvre and, I suspect, to all of modern poetry) is his translation of Callimachus's famous epigram attacking such Alexandrian contemporaries as Apollonius of Rhodes for their cyclic, or late secondary-epical poems. Callimachus's poem connects erotic longing with writing and erotic loss with the loss of originality: it is an early example of the echo-poem, in which an echo mockingly deconstructs and undermines a pathetic utterance:

> Detesting the popular novel, I fail to derive any pleasure
>> From such a byway as this which the many frequent.
> Heartily loathing a flibbertigibbet love-object, I never
>> Drink from the tap; I despise what is common or mean.
> Yes, I admit you are handsome, Lysanias, terribly handsome:
> Echo improves on the epithet "—and some one else's!"

The solution to the problem of translating Callimachus's *"kalos, naichi kalos"*—the term for a beautiful athlete so common it is found on vases—and the nasty echo that finds lurking in the almost "common or mean" term the word *allos* ("other"—the "someone else") is brilliant, although Hine plays it down by not italicizing "*and* someone else's," allowing the echo-joke to rise up gently through the almost casual, but high, tone.

It would be perhaps too easy to make a case for Hine as our most representative Alexandrian himself, but that would have little meaning unless it were made clear that it was the Alexandrianism of our entire age, the condition sometimes misleadingly called "postmodern," that he exemplifies. A fine classical scholar and translator of the minor Homerica and of Theocritus, the author of seven books of verse and a most remarkable long poem called *In and Out,* as yet only privately published, his body of work is altogether impressive even at the age of forty-three. Certainly the major anglophone Canadian poet of his generation (only Jay Macpherson can at moments come up to his blend of skill and power), he has been a resident alien in Europe and, particularly, in this country for the past seventeen years. That he has not been highly enough acclaimed is, given the situation of literature in verse in this country today, unremarkable. For "the popular novel" in his Callimachus version we may read "the popularly novel" and the tired academicisms it stands for in American and British poetry. Hine does not write for idiots or illiterates, who increasingly have come to make up the audience and the judges of contemporary verse. A reviewer barely able to grasp the fact that something very complex may be going on in the rhetoric of these poems will only conclude that something is being put over on him or her, and on what poetry should be. And the notion that something very important may be being done *by means of what is going on* will be inaccessible to such a reviewer, with no sense of anything in literature but performance, signification being forbidden ground. It is a travesty of reportage merely to point out the operations of Hine's wit, the enormous success of his control of accentual-syllabic lines and rhyming, without indicating what they are doing to and for the vision of human life that this splendid body of poetry calls up. As for all important poets, form is not a matter of style—as it is for most polemicists of form—but of a reconstructed ground of language itself. It provides a vocal range, a set of givens as important for the poet as a theology. Even more, its very uses and occasions must continually provide parables and fables in themselves of that toward which poetry is always pointing.

In his "Vowel Movements," for example, the twelve-line stanzas are made to move through the domains of twelve different vowel sounds: in each stanza, the same vowel occurs on almost every stressed syllable throughout, so that each "region" of the poem is like a region or state or condition of language itself, another domain of experience. And it gets to the very guts of the notion of condition, of inner state: the poem's own dynamic, a peristaltic journey, which takes the poet and the reader through the convolutions of its own bowel-vowels, is constantly being glossed along the way. Hine is too serious a writer not to allow his most masterful playing to raise ultimate questions, and "Vowel Movements" continually considers its own gestation, not so much regarding its own beauty in a mirror, but looking through it toward what lies beyond. In the /ay/ stanza, he can contemplate the false versions of what he has himself striven to design:

> "Highly stylized" politely describes the bright eyesores
>   Shining like diamonds or rhinestones in the night sky,
> Lifelike, provided life survives its vital cycle
>   And the tireless indictment of time's diatribe,
> While mankind, sightless, frightened, like a child in twilight,
>   Dies of the devices it was enlightened by.

Here, the final line, with its echo of the Shakespearean autumnal sonnet's ending—"consumed with that which it was nourished by"—that turns the earlier heat into late light, ties up the metaphor of contrivance that it had forced itself, by the very means of its own contrivances, to consider. The *scheme* of assonantal domains, the figure, device, or pattern of such arrangement, becomes the basis for what is truly a *trope,* and the poem makes a parable of its own devices.

It is this aspect of Hine's formal powers that the commentator must confront, rather than their mere existence. Formal skill is, after all, a necessary but not a sufficient condition for poetic creation. One trouble with an age like the present, in which one would be grateful even for more well-written literary verse in the way of certain middle-aged British poets, is that it makes even the empty pocket seem promising because it at least has no hole in it. Daryl Hine is not to be praised for his learning, for his musical and rhetorical skill, but for the mental travel on which they launch him.

Even if Hine's translation of all of the poetry of Theocritus were not in itself a remarkable and distinguished book, the verse epilogue to it, in over 640 lines of beautifully modulated accentual English hexameters, would have to be singled out as one of the more noteworthy poems of recent years. Addressed to his third-century Alexandrian original, the verse essay touches on most of the matters a reviewer of Hine's splendid version would want to explore: the astonishing originality of Theocritus's bucolic pictures or "idylls"; the fruitful subsequent history of the revisionary consequences of these poems, their mythology, their kinds of allegorizing in the major fictional mode we call pastoral; the relations between complex, allusive, literary English; the theory of verse translation generally; literary eros; ancient and contemporary homosexuality; literary treatments of botanical fact; and much more. Throughout, he speaks to the Greek poet with deep affection, as well as with astonishingly broad and well-digested learning:

> Gnomic and always ironic, your moral was seldom in earnest.
> Nor were your morals. Your vices distinguish your virtue from
>   Virgil's
> Who, with a Latin solemnity followed your frivolous footsteps.

The masterful handling of the colloquial rhythms of modern American speech and prose (by no means the same) in the hexameter framework is made even more masterful by the display of skill at what Samuel Johnson called "representative versification," as in the last line quoted above, where Virgil's "Latin solemnity" has already been established by the close of the preceding line, with its "virtue from Virgil's" rhythmic-semantic phrase, and its momentary fiction that the two words are etymologically, and therefore essentially, connected, infecting each with the touch of the other.

The translations themselves are remarkable for the way in which the learning and the skill seem to surrender their domains to the empire of the ear, the total poetic sound always allowing the reader to understand that a good deal has been going on in the original that is at least being represented in the English. The outdoor symphony of the *locus amoenus,* as described by Simichidas, a persona for Theocritus himself, in Idyll VII, the famous account of the Harvest Home, is full of the later resonances of this topos in subsequent poetry, from Virgil to Walt Whitman and beyond:

> Over our heads many poplars and loftily towering elm trees
> Soughed as they stirred in the breezes, while nearby the
>   numinous water
> Laughed as it flowed from the caves of the nymphs with a
>   metrical chatter,
> Whilst all about in the shadowy branches the smoky cicadas
> Worked at their chirruping—they had their labour cut out for
>   them! Far off
> Out of the thick-set brambles the tree-frog croaked in a
>   whisper:
> Linnets and larks were intoning their tunes, and the wood-dove
>   made moan.
> Busy and buzzing, the bees hovered over the musical waters.

The Keats here in the "making moan," and the interpretive "musical waters" for the *pidax* or "spring" of the Greek (such springs and fountains having long been established as tropes of poetic eloquence) are entirely appropriate for so allusive and resonant a text to begin with, and the last line is at once more allusive and more accurate than the Tennysonian "And o'er the fountain hung the gilded bee" of Charles Stuart Calverley's 1860s version of this idyll.

Idyll VI, with its poetical contest between Daphnis and Damoetas, is splendid; so is the couplet-for-couplet bout of the mime in V, the great prototype of what jazz musicians called a "cutting session." In the epithalamium for Helen, Idyll XVIII, Dryden (one of Hine's few truly poetical predecessors in translating Theocritus into English) must let his style have its way:

> With Pallas in the loom she may contend,
> But none, ah none can animate the lyre
> And the mute strings with vocal souls inspire!
> Whether the learn'd Minerva be her theme,
> Or chaste Diana bathing in the stream;
> None can record their heavenly praise so well
> As Helen, in whose eyes ten thousand Cupids dwell.

Hine gives us something that will always be less dated, as well as more deeply neoclassical:

> Nobody cuts from her patterned, elaborate loom such a close-knit
> Web as she weaves with her shuttle between the immovable uprights.
> No one has such understanding of playing the lyre as she does,
> Singing in honour of Artemis, also of buxom Athena,
> No one like Helen whose glances are pregnant with every desire.

The spell that the girl Simaetha works with her jinxing conjuring wheel to bring her lover back to her in II has a famous problematic refrain, and Hine does wonderfully with it:

> First of all barley is burnt on the fire—will you sprinkle thickly,
> Thestylis? Idiot, where have your wandering wits taken wing to?
> Must I be made an amusement of even by you, dirty creature?
> Scatter the barley and say, "I am scattering Delphis' bones now."
> *Magical whirligig, fetch to my house my unfaithful beloved.*

Hine's previous translation of the Homeric hymns, while most impressive, had an Alexandrian cast to it. But Theocritus is clearly his poet, and he shows us how much he is our poet as well. It is not so much that he has had to contend with a tradition of translation (as the translator of Homer or Virgil must do), for aside from the splendid 1588 version of six of the idylls by an anonymous Elizabethan, Dryden's really fine version of Idyll XXVII, and some momentary felicities of Calverley and Leigh Hunt, he is the first poet of importance to attempt a version both learned and imaginatively potent. In an age in which versifiers translate into lame free verse poems from languages that they do not know how to read, employing prose cribs that they turn into unsounding cut-up prose, this book sets amazingly high standards.

Hine has no doubt suffered a want of attention that he might have attained without his own want of vulgarity, crudity, and the knowledge of what poetry is, but such attention is given by that majority of whom Frost observed that they would rather vote than think. His astonishing *In and Out* (—of the Roman Church, as well as the old in and out of sex), with its intertwined chronicles of sexual and religious vocations and conversions, might, if commercially published, momentarily gain him a "gay" constituency, but it would be a readership as trivial for his poetry as one that seized on that wonderful book-length narrative because it is written in blank anapestic trimeter—as if either "theme" (or "area of interest") or "form" were in itself any more central than the unwritten-upon lines of a notebook: they may be blue, or gray, widely or narrowly spaced, and so forth. But it is what is written on and between and, ultimately, by means, and by way of, them that matters. Poems may have subjects as well as objects, but it is what they make of them that provides what they are about. Literalists cannot perceive this, but literalists—the morticians of poetry—never could, whether they author or consume the sweet, empty light verse of the Hallmark greeting card, or the scarcely less empty dark verse—the almost universal modes of bad American vers libre—that help extend the power of the unvanquished goddess Dulness everywhere. There are very few poets as good as Daryl Hine, and almost none like him. At the end of even a minor visit to some amusing banlieu one is moved to hail this remarkable guide, a walking university, with the *"in lumine tuo videbimus lumen"* of one's former standing university, "in thy radiance we see light," or with the blunter *"lux et veritas"* of his present one. In any event, a more than ironic point of light against Dulness's universal darkness. It will not go out.

An Inevitable Plot

Anthony Hecht

It was with an unbounded admiration that I encountered in 1954 Anthony Hecht's newly published first book, *A Summoning of Stones*. His skill was astonishing. I remember being impressed at the time by the artful, imaginatively purposeful "Double Sonnet," and by "La Condition Botanique" and "The Gardens of the Villa d'Este," with stanza forms of a beautifully articulated sort (returning in other ways in poems I loved like "The Origin of Centaurs," also from this earlier period). And there was the remarkable "The Vow" (so central a poem—along with his later "Green: An Epistle"—in showing what was precisely wrong and unpoetic about what soon began to be called "confessional" poetry). And the brilliantly parodic "Divisions upon a Ground," whose agenda—the "ground" was Wallace Stevens on sex—he later acknowledged in retitling it "Le Masseur de Ma Soeur."

Noticeable also was the almost Horatian way in which he was able from the very first—as he has ever more adeptly remained—to move at once through long periodic qualified sentences and through intricate recurring stanzaic patterns and never seem either talky or essayistic. But it was the urgency of the matter, not the meter, that authenticated the powerful eloquence. Their stance, although not their diction, owed something to the post-1940 Auden. (I am thinking of an expository and interpretative responsibility, for example.) Certainly the introduction these poems gave me to the domain of the post-Miltonic fallen garden, the continuing meditation on the Bible

Review-essay of Anthony Hecht's *Flight among the Tombs* (Alfred A. Knopf, 1997) and on his work in general. From *Raritan* 17, no. 1 (summer 1997).

and so many of the proof-texts of antiquity, distinguished him among his contemporaries. And I was led to hear in his poems what our common teacher, Mark Van Doren, had invoked as "the noble voice." A *Summoning of Stones* was one of an astonishing group of first books that appeared over a five-year period—James Merrill, *First Poems* (1951); W. S. Merwin, *A Masque for Janus* (1952); May Swenson, *Another Animal* (1954); Adrienne Rich, *A Change of World* (1954); John Ashbery, *Some Trees* (1956)—books that meant so much for those who were still apprentices to their accomplishment. Hecht's poetry was tough, but not "difficult" in certain obvious ways, at least if one had some kind of ear for the rhetoric of allusiveness, to Shakespeare and the King James Version. And not only for specific references but for high tone. One only came to recognize much later an almost Stevensian audacity: the concluding poem cites some of the preceding poems in the book; they are being alluded to as mere examples in an examination of an underlying—again, quasi-Stevensian—figure called The Passionate Man.

This fine book was followed by *The Hard Hours* ten years later—Hecht has tended to write slowly, never littering the scene with throwaways—and then by *Millions of Strange Shadows* in 1977, and by *The Venetian Vespers* two years after that. Its title poem, a marvelous long dramatic monologue, constructs new modes of narrative irony for that celebrated nineteenth-century form, with a narrator who may be unreliable even to himself. "The Venetian Vespers" concludes with one of the most shockingly effective allusions en passant that I know of in poetry. The poem is revealed toward the end to turn among other things on a complication of paternity, and a question of what the speaker may know or think he knows about it. That speaker, who has come to Venice to live out the remainder of his life amid that city's relentless offerings to the eye, seems to be responding in some complex way to Othello's obsession with "ocular proof." And that speaker, whose magnificent detailed descriptions both of the telling scenes of his childhood in Lawrence, Massachusetts, and of the sinking city the weight of whose apprehension by poetry and painting are almost too heavy to be borne, is in some ways a poetic descendent of Browning's talkative half-listener to Galuppi's toccata. He may be only half-aware of what he is saying in the last line:

                    I look and look
As though I could be simply saved by looking—
I who have never earned my way, who am
No better than a viral parasite,
Or the lees of the Venetian underworld,
Foolish and muddled in my later years,
Who was never even at one time a wise child.

The suppressed second half of the proverb points to the half-acknowledged matter in the poem. (I suppose this, and the missing half-proverb of John Ashbery's "Soonest Mended," are the two most telling examples—working in totally different ways—of the power of this device.) Another matter, too: one does not tend to think of him as a visionary poet, and certainly not, as was previously observed, as "confessional." And yet he learned early on to master the narrative unfolding of moment of vision. There is "A Hill," about which J. D. McClatchy has written so well, and "Apprehensions," as well as the long later monologue from *The Transparent Man* called "See Naples and Die."

There are indeed echoes of Shakespeare in this poem and throughout his work, as in the title of *Millions of Strange Shadows* (a reference to Shakespeare's Sonnet 53), with its ancillary matter of the different meanings of *shadow*—from the natural optical occurrence of physical occlusion to an image or picture or even metaphor of any kind. But they are to be found almost everywhere. It is as if this language, and phrases from the King James Version of the Bible (as other poets in English in the past were full of Virgil; as for the KJV, it's hard to realize that the *voice* of that text has more or less vanished in our lifetime) were part of the vernacular for his poetic dialect. And increasingly throughout the life of his work, one hears the interplay of high diction and the intensely colloquial, the gift that he shares with his contemporaries Merrill and Ashbery for the apprehension of the resonances of colloquial phrases and even of levels of tone, fine-tuned and deployed by each of these poets in his individual ways.

Something else that has distinguished Hecht's work throughout his career is his inability and/or refusal to write a trivial poem, a piece of skillful, amusing, or even telling padding, his very personal mode of high seriousness—what Hecht has called in Elizabeth Bishop "an infinitely touching valor." Even the highest play of his wit always serves this mode, whether in his celebrated "The Dover Bitch," from which Matthew Arnold's poem has never quite recovered, or in the imaginative exuberance of the string quartet into which he turns the four lovers of *A Midsummer-Night's Dream* in "A Love for Four Voices," as well as the ringing tones of the voice of the speaker in Ecclesiastes. It is also there in his moral rage. Nietzsche says somewhere that "all truths for me are soaked in blood"; for Hecht this is true of many of his tropes, even as his poetic art is soaked in truth.

Flight among the Tombs (the flight of the title that of the bat, identified in a telling line of Christopher Smart) is his first book since *The Transparent Man*, which appeared, in 1990, at the same time as his *Collected Earlier Poems*. Its grandest, but by no means its sole, truly major achievement is a remarkable *Totentanz* or Dance of Death, entitled "The Presumptions of Death," moving through a series of twenty-two poems accompanied by woodcuts by Leonard Baskin. Each is entitled by the name of a persona or type of Death ("Death the Hypocrite," "Death the Scholar," "Death the Judge"—these are traditional roles—as well as "Death the Mexican Revolutionary," "Death the Oxford Don," "Death the Film Director," and so on). These poems continually use masks of one conception of Death for purposes of unmasking all human enterprise as Death's collection of puppets. And they deploy a wealth of verse patterns, from a formal villanelle to a magnificently handled free-verse mode based on the King James version of the biblical Hebrew line, with particular allusive reference, in "Death the Inquisitor," to Proverbs and Job. Here, his questions are only rhetorical (it's his power and resolve that are inquisitorial), speaking as if in rebuke, in this case to any mere personifier:

> Who shall number the generations of the microbe,
>> Or the engenderings of the common bacillus? . . .
> I abide the corruption of tungsten,
>> The decay of massed granite.
> I shall press to the core of every secret.
>> There is no match for my patience.

While the individual poems vary widely in their rhetorical modes and the images they employ, there is a common tone—at least to the way in which they all allow their speaker's true voice to emerge at the conclusion. It is almost as if, had there been a "Death the Accountant," his piece would have ended with the ominously resonant phrase "the bottom line." For that is what the closures of all these poems finally come down to.

From early on in his writing, Hecht has shown a deep feeling for Northern Renaissance engraving, and premonitions of the present poem appear to me now to lurk in a poem, from his first volume, called, half-self-mockingly, "The Place of Pain in the Universe." It was omitted, along with half of the poems in *A Summoning of Stones,* from his *Collected Poems.* It starts out by meditating upon a toothache, and then moving to a rueful sort of memento mori:

> An old engraving pictures St. Jerome
> Studying at his table, where a skull,
> Crowned with a candle, streams cold tears of wax
> On its bone features for the flesh it lacks,
> Yet its white complement of teeth is full
> While all its pain runs happily to loam.

While this wears its paradoxes more lightly than would his later work, it does seem to privilege Northern printmaking as eminently representing grim dark truths of eros and thanatos. Another early poem of some relevance is his "Song of the Beasts," as first evidence of handling an emblematic cycle, and under the grimmest of conditions: a cock, ape, dog, and viper, sewn up in a sack with a human parricide under Roman law, each speaks his stanzaic piece.

Another precursor of the new sequence may be found in an early poem from *The Hard Hours.* Called "Tarantula or The Dance of Death," it has a very Holbeinian Death speaking his piece in deftly choreographed stanzas, all but sapphic, save for the missing extra syllable at the line-ends:

> During the plague I came into my own
> It was a time of smoke-pots in the house
> Against infection. The blind head of bone
>   Grinned its abuse.

The first line's "came into my own" is repeated at several points, but never more tellingly than when broken up and punned upon syntactically—thanks to the stanza structure's mandated final short line—at the very end of the poem:

> Some, caught in these convulsions, have been known
> To fall from windows, fracturing the spine.
> Others have drowned in streams. The smooth head-stone,
> The box of pine,
>
> Are not for the likes of these. Moreover, flame
> Is powerless against contagion.
> That was the thick black winter when I came
> Into my own.

Earlier on, too, the poet had collaborated with artists: with Baskin, almost forty years ago in a series of poems and images of "The Seven Deadly Sins," in his superb translation of Voltaire's poem on the Lisbon earthquake, accompanied by Lynd Ward woodcuts, and in the Aesopian morals in couplet epigram he did to accompany some of Bewick's celebrated wood engravings of the fables. Hecht acknowledges this concern, and reveals a deep feeling for Renaissance iconography, in the poem from the cycle called "Death the Copperplate Printer," beginning

> I turn Christ's cross till it turns Catherine's wheel,
> Ixion's wheel becoming Andrew's cross,
> All four being windlass ways
> To press my truth full home, force you to feel
> The brevity of your days,
> Your strength, health's teeth's desire's and memory's loss.

The punning on "turn" (*rotate* + *turn into*) is more than merely local wordplay: it makes one see transformations of signs as one might imagine them in another system—say, that the final Printer here could multiply the power of "+" by "turning"— rotating it forty-five degrees—into "×." But this preliminary stage of design (the images, the emblems) in the poem work out through successive stanzas to a "turning" of the printmaker's press into a figurative winepress, and, inevitably, an all-too-literal sixteenth-century torture device.

And yet this poem's central figure, and its manipulation with and through the constructions of the stanzas, is very different from those in the other poems. It is not only in the relation of poetic form to rhetorical format (a song, a harangue, an argument, a mock-confession, for instance). There are also continued reminders that, no matter how far the wit may go, we must always return to the inevitable, to a trope that was waiting in the wings, as it were, all along. So "Death the Film Director" (in some ways a sharp turn on the Renaissance commonplace of the *theatrum mundi*) ends by speaking for what is almost a conceptual refrain for all the rest of the poems:

> This film has a large cast
> A huge cast; countless, you might almost say;
> And for them all, for every one of them,
> I have designed, with supreme artlessness,
> What could be called an inevitable plot.

These local inevitabilities—given the particular conceit—keep reasserting themselves; thus, "Death the Carnival Barker" can harangue the crowd with "We're known throughout the world as fair and square," and his last lines are those that conclude the whole sequence in that same mode. It will be noticed here that the stanza form, a quatrain stuffed inside a couplet envelope, itself reminds us that there are inevitable closures contracted for, forgotten, that must be redeemed: the final rhyme is so distant from the first one that it takes a second to realize that it had been inevitable and, in this last stanza of the poem, not merely a full rhyme but a repetition (the opening one had rhymed, in the same positions, *back* and *crack*):

> No one has ever asked for his money back!
> Geniuses, beauties, all the greatest wits
> Have been our patrons! Once the show's begun
> Small kids admitted for a mere two bits!
> Fear not, my friends! There's room for every one!
> Step forward, please! Make room for those in back!

The longest of the "Presumptions of Death," a two-part dramatic monologue called "Death the Whore," may in fact be the most remarkable single poem of the group. It alters the format of many of the others—Death playing a particular role—in that the speaker is a person who has died, a wretched prostitute addressing a lover of her youth. Rather than as an agent of dying, Death in this poem is a voice blended of memory and imagination, and it constructs a unique relation to the past of the reader-writer-author of the other poems in the series. It is one of Hecht's most powerful monologues.

But another matter has to lurk, for a powerfully contemporary poet, in the very conception of the whole cycle, namely that Death is not to be trifled with, and that all our representations of him are, indeed, of necessity, trifles. To this degree he is mocking the tradition of mockery, but from another perspective. Hecht knows well the terrifying passage from book 2 of *Paradise Lost* that describes Death thus:

> The other shape,
> If shape it might be called that shape had none
> Distinguishable in member, joint or limb,
> Or substance might be called that shadow seemed
> For each seemed neither . . .

Nobody who has known Death is in a position to describe him. Everything we tell of Death is a story, and the only deconstruction of the rhetoricity of all our stories could occur in the silence of the grave itself. But this is one of the suppressed matters that make this chatterbox Thanatos so powerful a monologuist.

There is even more to *Flight among the Tombs* than the Death sequence, and it exhibits a variety of modes. "Matisse: Blue Interior with Girls etc. etc." is an ecphrastic poem marking an interesting development from "At the Frick" (on a Bellini) in his very first book, and the elaborate meditation on a Renoir in "The Deodand" from *The Venetian Vespers*. In the Matisse poem, the very matter of ecphrasis doubles, in a very fluid free blank verse, with the question of the moralized image.

> Deep in their contemplation, the two girls,
> Regarding art, have become art themselves.
> Once out of nature, they have settled here
> In this blue room of thought, beyond the reach
> Of the small and brief ambitions of the flesh.

There is the wonderful, brief "To Fortuna Parvulorum" with its acknowledgment of "in what altered tones I hear today / The remembered words, *'Messieurs, les jeux sont faits,'* / That stirred me as a boy."

"The Whirligig of Time" translates Horace in a Catullan mode, quite different from Hecht's earlier versions of Horace in *The Venetian Vespers*—his adaptation of 1.1 and, even more audaciously, 1.5, the ode "to" and against Pyrrha on which the young Milton tried his hand with great success. What Hecht does is to keep Horace's cutting edge sharp by grinding the blade into a newly curved shape. And so with the version in the new book. In "A Ruminant," a schoolboys' dirty song about the sexual life of the camel is made to serve high wisdom through off-rhymes partaking of the first stanza's etymologizing *camel/gimel*.

And there is the "Proust on Skates" that gives this whole section of the book its title, and an elegy for James Merrill who, he says, did "actually disappear in the dead of winter / More perfectly than Yeats"—because his death was more hearsay than usual, Merrill having died in an Arizona hospital far from most of his friends. (And, of course, quoting Auden on Yeats; implying a sort of series, something like one of a sequence of musical *deplorations* or memorial compositions written by early Renaissance composers—Ockeghem for Dufay, Josquin Des Prés for Ockeghem, and so on.) This wonderful poem incorporates and refigures Merrill's major trope in *The Changing Light at Sandover,* implicitly acknowledging its relation to classical and Christian funerary elegy.

"A Pledge" is a ballade, very different in character from the "ballade-lament for the makers" of "Death the Poet" in the sequence. Aside from Hecht in these poems only Auden (in "The Sea and the Mirror"), Wilbur, and—surprisingly—W. S. Merwin in a lament for a lost dog (a turn, like "Death the Poet" on the *ubi sunt* of Villon), and one or two others have done serious ballades in more than half a century. Its refrain, "The air is sweetest that a thistle guards," is from an early poem of Merrill's called "Europe," which Merrill himself picked up again in "Variations," in his *First Poems*.

And then there is the remarkable villanelle called "Prospects." This French lyric form, eight of whose nineteen lines are composed of two repeated refrains, provided a favorite format for literary versifying in the later nineteenth century after it was introduced into English by Edmund Gosse in 1874. But it somehow found its way into the work of important modern poets: E. A. Robinson wrote a great villanelle ("The House on the Hill"); Auden wrote several; Dylan Thomas the memorable "Do Not Go Gentle"; Theodore Roethke two fine ones; William Empson two extremely influential ones, the second of which led to Elizabeth Bishop's celebrated "One Art." A thematic thread runs through these, in that most of them are concerned with coping with loss in one way or another. This is perhaps spooky, since the very first villanelle in our sense was written by Jean Passerat (1534–1602) with the refrain lines *"J'ai perdu ma tourterelle"* and *"Je veux aller après elle."* "All Out," one of the two poems in *The Presumptions of Death* whose title does not invoke a persona of Death, starts out

> This is the way we play our little game:
> While I count up to ten the others hide.
> Do what you will, it always ends the same.

and, in the way of the best modern villanelles, subtly varies the refrain, as for example by mentioning rather than merely using it at one point:

> Some seek the fragile garnitures of fame
> While some drop out, claiming, to salve their pride,
> "Do what you will, it always ends the same."

"All Out" is a beautifully constructed poem, and exploits the hidden agenda of Death lurking in repetition, underlined by the subtle but strong self-reference of the second refrain—the tercets of the poem all end "the same," the poem itself ends with it, and we all end the same way. The set piece form is here given the ad hoc interpretative significance of a figure in a Dance of Death: once again, in the hands of a true poet, a verse form becomes a deeply poetic mode.

But good as this poem is (it reminds me of the best of Auden, somewhat, save for the self-referential element), I find "Prospects" more remarkable. And not surprisingly, for among other things, it stands alone, instead of playing a role as a phase of an unfolding serial structure. The enjambment across its two first

lines that contracts the absolute abstract noun to a more prag-
matic adjective promises much more than wit:

> We have set out from here for the sublime
> Pastures of summer shade and mountain stream;
> I have no doubt we shall arrive on time.

The easy colloquial mode of the third line (what will be the
second refrain), and the consonantal identity of the two rhymes
(sublime/stream/time)—these signal a little post-Heraclitan alle-
gory all by themselves. The questing journey of the poem—
toward an aesthetic sublime that itself again allegorizes a moral
one—commences by looking forward from a point at which
most looks are backward, into memory. Like the previous
villanelle, it cannot avoid evoking the matter of both its and
every poem's own journey toward a conclusion. In this case it is
underlined by having to "work through" a pattern of relentless
repetition, whose traps are those of jingle, as well as by the
governing metaphors of way, path, route, itinerary, etc., which
have such significances lurking even in their vernacular usage.
But I must quote the rest of the poem entire:

> Is all the green of that enamelled prime
> A snapshot recollection or a dream?
> We have set out from here for the sublime
>
> Without provisions, without one thin dime,
> And yet, for all our clumsiness, I deem
> It certain that we shall arrive on time.
>
> No guidebook tells you if you have to climb
> Or swim. However foolish we may seem,
> We have set out from here for the sublime
>
> And must get past the scene of an old crime
> Before we falter and run out of steam,
> Huddled by doubt that we'll arrive on time.
>
> Yet even in winter a pale paradigm
> Of birdsong utters its obsessive theme.
> We have set out from here for the sublime;
> I have no doubt we shall arrive on time.

The finality of closure will always be somehow reached "on time," but this is not the Death of the series speaking, dealing from his stacked deck. This is rather a remarkable glimpse of what art can mean. The absorption in it can make any prospect, even when glimpsed from a point toward an end of a journey, seem as if seen from *nel mezzo del cammin*. It is having great imaginative work to do, like that of a major poet, that initially affords such a prospect, and it is the true work of poetry to point this out to the rest of us.

Hecht has always striven for, and has come in the last twenty years to perfect, a nobility of expression that is all the more important in a democracy. Poetry is a realm in which elegance supplies, rather than vitiates, power of the best kind—power to make and change, rather than (in the tunnel vision behind the current official palaver of academic literary or "cultural" studies) power over people.

Richard Howard

An Introduction

I first met Richard Howard in the spring of 1949, at Columbia, at an annual poetry contest, where he read a most expert poem about the memorials of Egypt (I remember admiring its very skilled vers libre, its historical perspective—romantic and modernist, strangely, at once—and its epigraph from Hegel). But we barely spoke on that occasion and it was not until later that year that we were introduced by a childhood friend of his from Cleveland with whom I was beginning to keep company. For the next forty-five years I have had the pleasure of his personal friendship and his literary company, and I am inexpressibly moved at the honor of introducing him tonight.

As is generally known, he has published ten volumes of poetry, his most recent, called *Like Most Revelations,* published this year. From his first book *Quantities* (1962) on, Howard's poetry has not, it must be admitted, addressed itself to readers who have never read, nor heard of, very much. His poetic world is one of what might be called a deeply rooted cosmopolitan. But in this it remains central to a major strand in American literature. I am reminded of the Walt Whitman who writes a poem like "Italian Music in Dakota," which is about hearing a regimental band playing transcriptions of Bellini and Donizetti in a frontier landscape ("Rocks, woods, fort, cannon, pacing sentries, endless wilds"), the elegant sound and the western site harmonizing so perfectly that "Nature, sovereign of this gnarled realm . . . Listens well pleas'd." While first British and, following, American

---

An introduction prepared for his Chancellor's reading for the Academy of American Poets, the Morgan Library, October 3, 1994; printed in *Poetry Pilot* (winter 1994–95).

romanticism had to call attention away from mere cultivation to the deeper and broader culture of nature, it is the nature of culture that we are reminded not to neglect by a handful of prophetic American poets of great importance—I would prefer not to call them "postmodern," the term having fallen into the wrong mouths. Richard Howard's work represents this aspect of our moment so very well, like some of his contemporaries—Wilbur, Ashbery, Merrill, Hecht, and the late Amy Clampitt and Howard Moss, for example.

Richard Howard is also a remarkable man of letters of a sort seldom seen in this country any more. I shouldn't simply say "aside from his poetry" here, because his translation and his criticism are hardly the work—as Milton said of his own prose—of the left hand; it is rather as if he held two pens in one hand. His contributions to the serious and important poetry of our time have reached beyond the body of his own writing. A poet always, he began his life as a published writer in a sort of masquerade, the only serious kind of ghost writing we have, called literary translation. Richard is a prodigious translator from French with an incredibly wide range of accomplishment, from the official strength of his translation of de Gaulle's memoirs to his championship of the avant-garde novelists of the 1950s (the authors of the so-called *nouveau roman,* like Alain Robbe-Grillet, Claude Simon, etc.), from his fine versions of some of the poetry of St.-Jean Perse to all the poems of Baudelaire's *Les Fleurs du mal,* and, most recently, to Proust's *Du Côté de chez Swann.* He has translated a good deal of Roland Barthes, with whom he was closely acquainted, and brought to English-speaking readers the work of fascinating writers like E. M. Cioran. As a translator of 150 or so books, he has never been merely a passive literary presence, executing well tasks set for him by publishers, and so forth, but rather has initiated projects himself, impelled by his wide reading and vast enthusiasms and energies.

Even more importantly, in the same year—just twenty-five years ago, I note with some kind of inexpressible sense of gain and loss—as his *Untitled Subjects,* Richard brought out his re-markable critical book, *Alone with America.* It contained individual essays on fifty American poets roughly contemporary with him (the second edition an updated revision with additions on each poet's later work), all enwrapped in his critical prose, lapidary, glittering with reflections of the prose style of later Henry James. The book's one great fault was an almost unforgivable omission resulting from its inability to deal with the poetry of Richard Howard. One is thankful that this bravura reticence is absent from his splendid critical anthology called *Preferences*, in which he included himself. A fascinating set of observations on the choices made by contemporary poets of poems from the past with which they felt a momentary affinity, in this volume each principal poem, poem from the past, and comment by Richard was accompanied by a photograph (by the late Thomas Victor) of the poet, not for the purposes of the coffee table, but in order to say something about modes of manifest and latent self-portraiture.

But there is a profound poetic difference between manifest and latent self-portraiture—between literal autobiography, full of facts and lies and rhetoric and self-deception—and the truer figuration of self that is most authentic, disclosing more for what it more obviously and trivially conceals. And here is a matter close to the heart of Howard's work. At a belated moment in our various phases of history—of various modernisms, of what had been enterprising America in its relation to the museum of Europe, of (indeed, and for whatever it may mean) the millennium—historical blindness is ever more endemic among us. History isn't taught much in schools; professors, no longer of literature, either deify it or deconstruct it out of discursive existence, or warp it for grossly political agendas. That Calliope might come in aid of Clio seems perplexing, for in the sixteenth century, poetry and history (as opposed, more recently to poetry and science) were considered contenders for acknowledgment of their different modes of truth-telling. Among poetry's other tasks is the one of reminding us—reminding our conscious capacities, even if only *en passant*—that closure to the past is a deadly kind of imprisonment. The point here is that Richard Howard is not only a poet of personality, but of history.

Ultimately, though, his work is most familiar to us through his—should we call them impersonations? no—for his is rather an art of what I'll call *personation:* having exemplary persons, actual or fictional but usually quite dead, return from the grave to tell us what they had never said before. That many of these figures are artists, writers, musicians, or powerful women associated with them is not to say that they are any less exemplary—Emerson called it "representative"—than warriors or governors, drudging hod-carriers or busy midwives.

Of these personations inhabiting a good part of his work, most are Europeans. But Howard always sings a particularly American note. In a significant portion of his work, this note is not that of the familiar poetic birds—skylark, nightingale, darkling- or hermit-thrushes—but rather our central American one. Richard Lewis, in his little-known remarkable poem of the 1730s called "A Journey from Patapsko to Annapolis," first established the central emblem of American poetic eloquence, the voice of belatedness that could nonetheless draw innovative power therefrom: outdoing the European nightingale (Milton's, and what would almost a century later be Keats's) is the American mockingbird.

> Oh, sweet Musician, thou dost far excel
> The soothing song of pleasing *Philomel!*
> Sweet is her Song, but in few Notes confin'd;
> But thine, thou Mimic of the feath'ry Kind,
> Runs thro' all Notes!—Thou only know'st them *All,*
> At once the *Copy,*—and th'*Original.*

The mockingbird, whether made so by Whitman directly, or by all of us allegorically, speaks to, for, and of the American poet.

Richard's first volumes were impressive for their extremely skillful, learned verse, with one remarkable poem, "An Encounter" in his second book, *The Damages,* perhaps looking forward to a power he would later display more generally. But the astonishing acts of creative ventriloquism in his justly acclaimed, Pulitzer Prize–winning *Untitled Subjects* (1969) manifested this throughout. It was a volume of dramatic monologues, each titled not by the name of a speaker, but by a date—Harold Bloom pointed to "their intricate blendings of our emergent sensibility and the anguish and splendor of the great Victorians." But I find on rereading his early work that "From the Remains of Count C.W.: after Rilke" and "Bonnard: A Novel" introduce us early on to the way that the genre of dramatic monologue would occupy a central place in his poetry. It was also in a second book that he began to explore the syllabic verse—a formal legacy from Marianne Moore and W. H. Auden—out of which he built his own inimitable metric within which to cast his marvelously ever-qualifying periodic syntax.

Starting out from where Browning left off—and from where Pound and Eliot never moved much further on—Howard developed a mode of dramatic monologue of remarkable ironic depth and brilliance, and which he has continued to explore. I might mention here my two most favorite poems in his book *Findings*—"November, 1889" and "The Chalk Cliffs of Rügen" (and this last combines two of his favorite genres, dramatic monologue and ecphrasis), the collection called *Two-Part Inventions,* and, after a number of books in which he explored the realm of photographic portraiture with his remarkable series of poems addressed to images by the French nineteenth-century photographer Nadar—the poems in his newest volume, *No Traveller.* Of those two poems in *Findings* I mentioned, it is significant that the monologuist of the first is Browning himself, arriving in Venice about a month before his death on the same day that his final volume, *Asolando,* was published. It is equally significant that the monologuist of the second poem is a figure in Caspar David Friedrich's celebrated painting, talking of himself and two more persons also in the scene; but the narration is so contrived that which of the three it is we can never know. Howard's poetry indeed frequently performs a brilliant ballet of such evasions. At the same time, in those personations issues of art and truth, power and detail, and ingenuity and terror always lurk large.

At his best, I would rank Howard among the finest of his contemporaries: Ammons, Merrill, Ashbery, Merwin, Strand, Hecht, the late May Swenson and Howard Moss; but his poetic oeuvre has been somewhat diluted by a good deal of very clever and serious verse, far more engrossing—for someone of any literary and artistic culture and active intellect—than most piously solemn and sincerely "deep" verse by most putative poets, but still not up to his own snuff. The most recent book, I feel, was really splendid. I can in no way predict where his poetry will go, but it is—as he might put it—so unquestionably *there* that I find it impossible to believe that it will die, and that he won't go on doing astonishing things. I'm just not certain as to whether he will continue to mark time or not (but he is at an age at which one doesn't have that much time to mark).

Alone with America's critical prose seems ultimately designed to avoid committing itself to any kind of clear position. When it's good, his critical writing can point to interesting things in the writer's work, but Howard never writes as a teacher, and he isn't sufficiently interested in the grounds of judgment to justify sufficiently his tendency to avoid it. Nonetheless, you can't read about in that massive book without getting a very good sense of what the work of each poet in question is like, even if Howard will never let you know how good, how important (even to himself), how interesting (depending upon what you're interested in) each poet is. His other critical work has shared these virtues and faults (see his interesting observations on the choices made by contemporary poets of poems from the past with which they felt a momentary affinity in *Preferences*). But in any event, given his energy, enthusiasm, unwavering commitment to knowledge in literature and art and to the moral necessity of knowledge of history, he couldn't help but be magnificently exemplary. His poetry deploys so well the art of *explaining* that anything further to be said of it would be supererogatory. It will now speak for—in—and, ventriloquially *by*—itself.

In Memoriam
James Merrill

It was early in 1952, at the apartment of a common friend (whom neither of us saw during the last few decades) that I first met James Merrill. He was carrying a copy of his *First Poems;* I soon became even more in awe of it than I had been of their author, with whom on that occasion I exchanged no more than a few totally forgotten words. Quite properly, it was the poems, not the poet, that left their mark on me. (And I can actually remember the copy of the book—with its golden jacket and white lettering designed by the great designer Harry Ford, who would become the editor of subsequent books not only by James but of so many other poets as well—better than I can now recall the poet's face as it was then, and which I constantly need old photographs to retrieve.) What struck me first wasn't what would now be re-marked on upon as the technical mastery of verse, for in those days, most writers who presumed to be poets had the skills needed for such mastery. (It must be remembered of course that, whereas not having the skills prevented you from being a poet, having them didn't make you one.) In Merrill's *First Poems,* it was the fine ear for the cadences of English, and the nuances of tone that the handling of accentual-syllabic meter and deftly orchestrated rhyming were always modulating like a present voice. It was the voice of a storyteller and soliloquizer who somehow never stopped being a conversationalist, and whose stories and reflec-tions were never baldly about himself but about his listeners (and if they didn't realize that at the time, they would come to know it,

---

Part of this was written for and read at a commemorative ceremony for James Merrill at the New York Public Library, May 13, 1995; with some additions, from *Poetry* 166, no. 6 (September 1995).

either in the course of the listening, or, deliciously, later). It was easy immediately to admire the beautiful use of complex stanza-patterns, or the handling of rhymed pentameter triplets in the three last poems of that book. In particular, the cadences of Andrew Marvell's favorite octosyllabic eight-line stanza, which have entranced generations of American poets from Emerson on, emerged marvelously for me in Merrill's "Poem in Spring," with its shadows of Robert Frost at the end, and its brilliant repossession of the proverbial "not being able to see the forest for the trees" at the end of the first stanza:

> Being of earth, we've come to sit
> On fecund ground, and fondle it—
> A filial diversion this.
> Then brother-sisterly we kiss
> Who cannot tell one branch for buds
> Nor see, for trees, the April woods
> Cloudy with green, nor amorous,
> Think autumn looks askance at us.

Twenty years after, James himself characterized the writing of these poems as "having fed / Feelings genuine but dead / With language quick but counterfeit." But here, perhaps with every right, but no reason, he sells himself a bit short, for to call this language counterfeit implies that there is a legitimate coin of the realm stamped with the king's real face. But the only kings in the realm of poetry are false claimants, and it is only when the poet can stamp whatever metal with his or her own profile that the coin rings true. Even as this "derivative" poem sits on and fondles the fecund ground of the great poetry of the past, the diversion itself will be truly of filiation, and the ground will bring forth what is green.

I suppose that it was the poem called "The Black Swan," though, that totally consumed me: that marvelous meditation on the bird whose "arched neck is like a question-mark on the lake" begins by considering the

> splendor
> That calls the child with white ideas of swans
> Nearer to that green lake
> Where every paradox means wonder . . .

It is that wonder in which poetry and philosophy both begin and in which they both remain before going their separate ways, before doing different things with the matter of wonder. We are all children with white ideas of swans before poetry makes the black swans happen, by seeing them on the green lake where for prose they are simply not, or by painting the white ones black from memory: certainly the poet must have green ideas of lakes in order to put it all together.

For me, putting the poetry and the poet all together would take a good while. It wasn't until the winter of 1957–58 that I reencountered this marvelous poet and perfect friend in New London, Connecticut. It was not until the following year that I first heard him read—from his second book, *The Country of a Thousand Years of Peace*—the remarkable poem called "Mirror." Hearing it was electrifying. The poet's fine way of reading taught us all there at the time not only how to read the poem, but something more general about how poems read aloud, and about how, with language quick but not counterfeit, they pay so handsomely for the attention they command. James was one of the most skilled and affecting public readers of his own poetry I had heard. There are writers of verse—now, more than ever—who, before an audience, chant or drone or strut or mince or yammer or harangue, but very few can read their work so as to keep their listeners constantly aware of the beauty of sense, however complex, and the sense of beauty arising from the powerful, delicate, and compelling ways in which that sense is made by poetry. Whether in a small room to two or three people—as I remember hearing the staggeringly beautiful "Lost in Translation" from him before I had read it—or before the largest of audiences, James Merrill was, as I say, among the very few great performers of poetry I have ever encountered. The sound of his reading voice lies continuingly inscribed for me—as that of Auden and Frost—in the texts of his poems. One hears him now as one reads him.

I had no idea when I heard "Mirror" then how future literary historians would view this poem as well as some others: I could mention the various "short stories" that looked forward to his almost lifelong substitution of poems for novels (indeed, "The Book of Ephraim" which introduces the whole of *The Changing Light* at *Sandover* is itself, you may remember, the replacement for an incomplete novel the ms. of which the author actually lost in a taxi). Or "Hall of Mirrors" or "The Charioteer of Delphi" or the more literally prophetic "Voices from the Other World," where, after nightly sessions at the Ouija board that produce babbles of voices, the speaker, relieved by the ordinary noises of the time being, avows that those voices are still

> clamoring overhead
> Obsessed or piteous, for a commitment
> We still have wit to postpone
>
> Because, once looked at lit
> By the cold reflections of the dead
> Risen extinct but irresistible,
> Our lives have never seemed more full, more real,
> Nor the full moon more quick to chill.

It is not only the whole realm of hell, purgatory, and paradise of Merrill's later major poem that is being proleptically awaited here, but rather the question of how poets know of memories they haven't had yet, of events that have happened but not to them. Of course, there has been something trivially sensational about the matter of a Ouija board that could be so magnificently oracular and—unlike the Delphic oracle that Herodotus said always spoke in hexameters—lend itself so magnificently to such elegantly complex kinds of translation. Sublime mountain revelations, voices in forests, glimpses of arpeggios of islands—all sorts of places in which poets have in the past been made aware of what was to be said—all evolve in time; Merrill's is a domestic scene of revelation, a household, an inverted teacup closing its mouth (or ear?) to present chatterings and opening itself to silent voices of memory.

Thus the matter of belief for James Merrill's poetry does not arise from inquisitorial journalistic questions about the sources of imaginative instruction; not belief "in" the power of Ouija boards to produce discourse—which is no more problematic after all than the power of trays to hold teacups. It is rather something far more secret and arcane, and yet generally accessible to anyone without even minimal hardware. For poetry, in fact, the most enabling of beliefs is in the inner power of language itself.

But the voice of his poetry remains present and need not procedurally be summoned up. It was, as was said before, always the voice of a storyteller. The two major poets of this century who preceded him (and how very differently!) in the matter of the poetic revision of prose narrative—Hardy and Robert Penn Warren—were both novelists who turned in their major later work to verse. James had indeed written three novels. The first was his somewhat autobiographical roman à clef, *The Seraglio* (1957); the second was a brilliant experimental novel—a novel *en abîme* like Gide's *The Counterfeiters,* Doris Lessing's *The Golden Notebook,* or Albert Memmi's *The Scorpion*—called *The (Diblos) Notebook* (1965). The final prose fiction was to have been a novel based on twenty-five years of his and David Jackson's communion through the medium of the Ouija board with those voices of the past that come to poets in so many varied ways. As is well known to his readers, the ms. of what had been written of that book was lost in a taxicab in Atlanta, and the story of its loss recorded in a poem called "The Will." Subsequently, a complex poetic narrative of twenty-five hundred lines, "The Book of Ephraim," replaced it and eventually emerged as the first part of his wonderful trilogy, *The Changing Light at Sandover.* But perhaps it is the general figure of a poem replacing a story that generates so much of Merrill's poetry.

Merrill was a poet for whom lyric inevitably engaged narrative, whether as—in the way D. G. Rossetti put it—"a moment's monument," or in the much harder way of connecting such small monuments to each other so that they may still be true, in some way, to time. This is not like stringing beads but more like—as Merrill himself suggested in an important earlier poem, "The Thousand and Second Night"—the vital task of Scheherazade under imminently mortal circumstances. He was able to make of the long poem something whose possibility all the dogmas of modernism denied—an unflaggingly imaginative work whose incidents and elements were connected not with string but with a substance spun from their own immortal diamond. A Merrill narrative has always been a tale whose telling told tales on ordinary telling itself. Merrill's poems suffer from neither the ugliness of beads strung too far apart on nasty-looking wire, nor of the hit-and-run effect of epigrams that too hastily leave the scene of their rhetorical accident. Whenever his frequent flashes of wit catch our eye, they come from the mirroring facets of a remarkable gem.

It is odd that so much has been made of Merrill's calling up the voices of the dead directly in *The Changing Light at Sandover,* since whenever we read a great novel or play we hear the voices of the characters, and when reading a moral or philosophical essay we hear the voice of the author. Our original versions of the past all speak to us in their own ways. The classical Muses gave way first, with poets like Dante and Petrarch, Milton and Spenser, to more potent goddesses, either compounded out of the remarkable fabric of white lies about what was autobiographical and what was not, or in the two Protestant poets, suitably and potently internalized as private goddesses within. For Pope the muse was a partially draped figure who made a good show of claiming to be Truth. Neoclassical chatter has always had it that separate Muses presided over separate musicopoetic modes and genres; Blake hated them not because they were claimed as sponsors by just such chatter, but purported that it was because they were the daughters of Memory. He utterly banished the Muses, daughters of hateful, mechanical Memory, in favor of the daughters of Imagination.

But some time between the writing of Wordsworth's *The Prelude* at the turn of the nineteenth century and the writing of Proust's *A la Recherche du temps perdu* in our century, a new Memory was born, involuntary, grandmotherly, and sometimes brotherly (for it was also in the nineteenth century that the muse first cross-dressed, as Arthur Hallam for Tennyson and Shelley for the young Browning). Merrill's muse was this very figure of later Memory, herself the great-great-great-great granddaughter of Calliope. She was not Calliope—as Muse of epic narrative—or Clio, Erato, or Thalia, nor even, as would seem far more likely, their mother, Mnemosyne. Rather, she was a post-Blakean figure, neither classic nor romantic, whom we might only awkwardly and chiasmatically call Memory Imagined/Imagined Memory. The poetry she mandated had that amazing power which we now too casually associate with fractals—the power seemingly to represent, in various scalar levels of its minutiae, its larger rhythms and movements.

That muse sang to him—which is to say that his poetic genius worked for him—in powerful and subtle ways. It is not only in the kind of poetic storytelling that re-members dismembered moments of what are, after all, the whole bodies of our lives, but something more than that. Since classical times, it has been understood that painters, to create the fictive space in which two-dimensional projections will whisper of a third, must employ shadows—themselves painted shadows of cast shadows—in order to create modeled forms. In general, Poetry's shadows are those of trope, the nonliteral senses of words and their relation to other words they look and sound like. It is this "ulteriority," as Robert Frost called it, this saying one thing and meaning other, that gives poetry its kind of truth. But every poet has his or her own particular palette of shadows as well. James's pictures of what is were always shadowed by what was, what was being, what has and had been; and the wonder of it all is how those shadows are not deadening, but quickening, affording flat tale-telling the truth of roundedness.

His whole life in art was true—in another sense—to that truth. He was always a wonderful teacher of the sort that, like Frost's ovenbird, "knows in singing not to sing," a quiet tutor without podium or pulpit. He and his work were of course skeptically reluctant about such a role. To this degree he was like the pier-glass in his "Mirror" poem, to which I shall return in a moment.

Merrill was always quickening yet again the already living language, and the wordplay that marked his writing and his astonishing conversational improvisation—he was more brilliantly funny than anyone I've known well—was always a kind of noble word-work. So that when he spoke in one poem of "that same old story / Father Time and Mother Earth, / A marriage on the Rocks" he is at once talking of titanic personages and—through the poem's previously implied citation of the old "Time is Money"—his own family. His wit always hovered between the deeply lyrical and the momentarily epigrammatic, and always beautifully easy. But the way of his work was never that. "I trust I am no less time's child than some / Who on the heath impersonate poor Tom / Or on the barricades risk life and limb" he went on to say in that same poem, "The Broken Home," reminding us that there are aspects of our lives in which to be on the barricades is indeed to be on the sidelines. Exemplary always was his refusal (or was it merely a blessed inability?) to—as his friend

Wystan Auden put it—"ruin a fine tenor voice for effects that bring down the house."

The retrieval of lost childhood, the operations of voluntary and involuntary memory (and of an imaginative memory even more mysterious), the mutual impersonations of life and art—the importance of these in his work kept making it increasingly apparent, as that work unfolded, how present Marcel Proust remained for him. Jimmy paid manifest homage to Proust in various ways in the course of his writing, such as the undergraduate thesis he wrote on him at Amherst and, of course, the wonderful anecdotal "For Proust" in *Water Street* in which "What happened was becoming literature." Not to speak of his institution of the *Balbec Liederbuch*—to which he got several friends to contribute—of Proust songs, quasi limericks on some Proustian theme or moment to be sung to the tune of "Colonel Bogey" (then recently popularized because of its prominence in a film called *The Bridge on the River Kwai*). What I remember as Jimmy's opening contribution went:

> *Swann's Way* (pause) a book by
> Mar-cel Proust—
> Tells how (pause) its hero
> Took to roost
> Racy
> Odette de Crécy
> To whom his friends could
> Not be in
> Troduced.

But I want to recall here that poem called "Mirror" I mentioned before, which is more obliquely, but deeply Proustian. It is also, as I mentioned previously, one of the very first poems I ever heard him read, thirty-eight years ago in New London. This haunting and prophetic monologue is spoken by a reflective pier-glass across a room from a merely transparent window, and propounds a meditation on memory and imagination. From the beginning, I thought of the speaker, the mirror, as a sort of wise old Proustian aunt, acknowledging questions of childhood and age, the reconstruction of life by art, and of her own lapse into final transparency.

I grow old under an intensity
Of questioning looks. *Nonsense,*
I try to say, *I cannot teach you children*
How to live.—If not you, who will?
Cries one of them aloud, grasping my gilded
Frame till the world sways. *If not you, who will?*

But the children who peer into the mirror, the children with bright ideas of mirrors and of life, are right. Like the mirror, this whole poem, James Merrill's poetry, and—most remarkably—his entire life, have been exemplary for so many writers of our time, in what they teach. It is by example, not precept, that we have learned these things from him: Remember to remember, that you not succumb to the nostalgias. Remember that the beauty with which language can clothe herself causes the truth of life to disrobe; that wit is knowing, and is often more generous than solemnity. Remember that certain truths can only be sung; that what has been broken in one way can only be made whole in another. Remember that to say with Proust that desire engenders belief is not to say with ambiguous ancient Wisdom that love is blind. Love knowingly. Know lovingly. And squander nothing.

A Word about Kenneth Koch

The appearance of Kenneth Koch's *Selected Poems, 1950–1982* is a long-overdue pleasure, and although those who admire his work as much as I do cannot help but regret certain favorites among his earlier poems that got lost in selection, this volume is of great value. It will allow unfamiliar readers to perceive, and knowing ones to reflect upon, the consistency of a joyful and energetic mode through over thirty years of, given that consistency, amazingly unrepetitive writing. Koch's continuing celebration of the playful sublime has always constituted a sort of gaudy tent, pitched among the ruins of high seriousness; a welcome sight in the intense heat, it has dispensed souvenirs and guidebooks (not to the ruins, but to itself) and orange juice, frequently blue in color, with such diligence and reliability that one has finally come to realize that the classical ruins were only random rubble, and that the tent was one of the unnamed goddess's authentic temples after all. The tent was striped with the bright, old colors of the New: Ariosto's proclaimed intention of writing of *cosa non detta in prosa mai, ne in rime*—what had not been said in prose before, nor verse—was inscribed on balloons in bunches. That the poet's true originality soared higher than those balloons of French modernist and *avant-gardiste* novelty may not have been discernible to most of the tourists over the years; this was, given the eternal nature of poetic reception, almost inevitable. But this lovely book should enable readers to participate more knowingly in the celebrations.

Koch's favorite kind of poem seems to be the set of variations, and the variation structure is itself varied and revised throughout his work. The first poem of his I ever read (in 1957?) was the

---

In part from *Partisan Review* 27, no. 2 (spring 1960), in part from *Yale Review* 74, no. 4 (summer 1985) with some additions.

wonderful "The Artist," a sort of visionary journal and scrap-book of a sculptor whose projects evolve from steel cigarettes and a cherrywood avalanche to a scheme of almost global pro-portions. Here, for example, is Koch's artist in re the question of *Bee:*

Pittsburgh, May 16th. I have abandoned the steel cigarettes. I
  am working on *Bee.*
Bee will be a sixty-yards-long covering for the elevator shaft
  opening in the foundry sub-basement
Near my home. So far it's white sailcloth with streams of golden
  paint evenly spaced out
With a small blue pond at one end, and around it orange and
  green flowers. My experience in Cleveland affected me so
That my throat aches whenever I am not working at full speed. I
  have never been so happy and inspired and
Play seems to me now like a juvenile experience!

❧

June 8th. *Bee* is still not finished. I have introduced a huge
  number of red balloons into it. How will it work?
Yesterday X. said, "Are you still working on *Bee?* What's
  happened to your interest in steel cigarettes?"
Y. said, "He hasn't been doing any work at all on them since he
  went to Cleveland." A shrewd guess? But how much can they
  possibly know?

❧

November 19th. Disaster! *Bee* was almost completed, and now
  the immense central piece of sailcloth has torn. Impossible
  to repair it!
December 4th. I've gone back to work on *Bee!* I suddenly
  thought (after weeks of despair!), "I can place the balloons
  over the tear in the canvas!" So that is what I am doing. All
  promises to be well!
December 6th. The foreman of the foundry wants to look at my
  work. It seems that he too is an "artist"—does sketches and
  watercolors and such. . . . What will he think of *Bee?*

Plans, doubts, hopes, fears, the whole paraphernalia of confi-dences in any artist's or writer's book of *son coeur mis a nu,* surround the records of the creation and reception of what would look today like a series of examples drawn from the fashionable art of the past two decades. But this poem was not "influenced" by pop art; rather, so much of the framing of both objects and hunks of environment which went on subsequent to its publication seem to have been dully literal, even if unwitting, illustrations of it. (Here the relation of true poetry to false art perhaps mirrors that of art to nature: Whistler was once accosted by a lady who remarked that she had been walking on the Embankment and that the Thames looked just like one of his *Nocturnes,* to which the artist replied that Nature seemed to be creeping up.) The elements of Koch's artist's oeuvre were mythological and paradigmatic, with the result that they became, in this Whistlerian-Wildean sense, literally prophetic. "The Artist" is one mode of variation on the variation theme, the "what next?"- ness that such patterns inevitably engender being tied here to the narrative of an artistic career. From the early *Collected Poems* to the more recent *In Bed,* Koch is at work on what will be next. The hilarious and beautiful "Lunch" from his first book is itself a Banquet of Sense, what used to be called a "travelogue" of exotic lunches. I quote from one of them as an instance of the author's superb ear and rhythmic timing:

> O launch, lunch, you dazzling hoary tunnel
> To paradise!
> Do you see that snowman tackled over there
> By summer and the sea? A boardwalk went to Istanbul
> And back under his left eye. We saw the Moslems praying
> In Rhodes. One had a red fez, another had a black cap.
> And in the extended heat of afternoon,
> As an ice-cold gradual sweat covered my whole body,
> I realized, and the carpet swam like a red world at my feet
> In which nothing was green, and the Moslems went on praying,
> That we had missed lunch, and a perpetual torrent roared into
>   the sea
> Of my understanding. An old woman gave us bread and rolls on
>   the street.

The whole poem concludes with a consideration of, and a gleeful escape from, the problems raised by its own injunction. "Let us give lunch to the lunch." Both the problems and the injunction itself are more in the line of S. J. Perelman—one of the major unavowed influences on the fiction and poetry of a whole generation of American writers—than of French poetry. Koch's ongoing homage to Ariosto, in the ottava rima of his narrative poems *Ko* and *The Duplications* (alas, not included in this section: who could ever forget the opening of the former of these, the only epic or romance ever *literally* to begin in media res with the word "Meanwhile"?), is matched by his continual delight in the tones of poems like Whitman's "Respondez" or "Apostrophe," and in the parable that his free verse is always preaching about itself, in what is really a very neoclassical way of moralizing, as Pope did from the form and function of his couplets, about lines of life from lines of verse. Koch's characteristic scheme of apostrophe, particularly of long and awkwardly named things and beings, is perhaps ultimately Whitmanic as well, but only in style. More deeply, it may have been a poem like (but I suppose that there isn't any other poem "like") Stevens's "Someone Puts a Pineapple Together" that helped Koch see what there was to be seen; even more than the more obvious format of the "Thirteen Ways of Looking at a Blackbird," the series of exuberant misreadings of the pineapple on the table in the shaft of light from the planet of the imagination falling upon it remains a rhythmic model for his sequences of surprising verbal moves.

Koch's early (1960) *Ko, or a Season on Earth* is, as I mentioned before, not included in this volume. But it is worth considering in the light of his later work. It is a long, very funny, mock-heroic poem in five cantos of ottava rima, dealing with, but mostly digressing from, the rookie season with the Brooklyn Dodgers of a young Japanese pitcher of talents scarcely to be believed. The very first line is programmatically mock-epical, dutifully opening the poem strictly, by the book, in medias res, with a kind of ingenuous deadpan literalness: "Meanwhile at the University of Japan / Ko had already begun his studies" begins Koch, with nary an invocation of the muse. "Meanwhile," however, remains his favorite word throughout the poem, robustly shoving the divers episodes into their lines in a kind of narrative relay-race, guiding the reader about the face of the globe whereon the action rambles, substituting for structure and maintaining a semblance of order. These various episodes involve the adventures of, among others, a British proletarian named Huddel; a private detective named Andrews; a kind of Sax Rohmer international manipulator with a fixation on dogs; and a poet named Joseph Dah who is not content with metaphor but demands in life and art a real *becoming*—Koch calls him an "action poet," and, as his daughter Doris explains to her lover Andrews as her father rushes into the cabin of a yacht in the form of a dog,

> Dad's integrity
> Makes him, unlike most poets, actualize
> In everyday life the poem's unreality.
> That dog you saw on deck with steel-gray eyes
> Was but a creation of Dad's terrible musical potency.
> Then seeing the dog there made him realize
> That the dog was himself, since by himself created,
> So in this poem it's incorporated!

(Even this stanza, by the way, reveals some of the poem's most common resources in the near Miltonic parody of the penultimate line as well as in the strained gag-like humor in the "I-don't-care-if-it-doesn't-rhyme-or-scan-very-well-the-last-three-words-are-a-*riot*" quality of the fifth one.) The plot of the whole poem keeps cross-cutting from one of these stories to another, returning to Ko and the Dodgers and a crucial game with Cincinnati from time to time, and every once in a while bringing two or more of its strands in a deliberately overcontrived fashion, while Koch crows with delight over the coincidences he has engineered. The poem's narrative technique must be traced back to Ariosto, I think, rather than merely to Byron (who is, of course, obviously present here and there); the comic impulse is more toward a rich, zany riot of improbability than toward the embodiment of a satiric perspective in Don Juan's peculiar kind of innocence, for example. The confrontation of innocence and experience in various forms is present throughout *Ko*. But it is always used for local humor and never as a basic conceptual framework for the narration. The characters in this poem have no inner lives at all—perhaps Koch's reversal of Rimbaud for his subtitle constitutes a kind of declaration of war on most contemporary writers' notions of what experience is. In general, though, it is never the poem's comic mechanism.

I think that it would be a mistake to compare *Ko* with, say,

Auden's *Letter to Lord Byron*, which is much more of a brilliantly skilled pastiche, and, in its way, very much more serious. Koch's successes are of a different sort, and occur whenever *Ko* erupts most naturally into imaginative excesses. My favorite episode occurs in the first canto after Joseph Dah has locked his daughter and her lover in a coffin and thrown them into the sea:

> Meanwhile in Kansas there was taking place
> A great upheaval. High school girls refused
> To wear their clothes to school, and every place
> In Kansas male observers were amused
> To see the naked girls, who, lacking grace,
> Were young, with bodies time had not abused,
> And therefore made the wheatfields fresher areas
> And streets and barns as well. No matter where he is
>
> A man is cheered to see a naked girl—
> Milking a cow or standing in a streetcar,
> Opening a filing cabinet, brushing a curl
> Back from her eyes while driving in a neat car
> Through Wichita in summer—like the pearl
> Inside the oyster, she makes it a complete car.
> And there were many sermons on the subject,
> And autoists, come in to have the hub checked
>
> On their old car, would stand and pass the day
> With talking of the various breasts and waists
> They'd seen throughout the week, and in what way
> They thought the thing, according to their tastes,
> Was right or wrong, that these young girls should stray
> Through Kansas without even stocking pastes
> Upon their legs . . .

As can be readily seen, Koch attains no "answerable style" here: he is often trapped into Ogden Nashisms or worse; half the time he triumphs over his demanding stanza form in expounding the story as he has obviously wanted to, the other part of the time using the form only to abuse it and to let it snarl back and take bites out of his story. He commits himself to a name for a character solely because of the exigencies of rhyme (a coach named De Bruins only enters the scene to rhyme with "ruins," but remains on throughout the poem, growing no more real at each mention of him). The stanzas are seldom end-stopped. One of the characters, we learn, had great skill "In juggling figures and in making millions. / At seventeen he joined the firm of Trillians, Trillians, Trillians, Trillians, Trillians, Trillians, / Trillians, Tull and Trillians, Limited." But all this is calculated irresponsibility. The whole poem is quite like Terry Southern's indescribable novel *Flash and Filigree,* in making a point out of keeping something up longer than could be believed possible. In going nowhere it stops at some outlandish and hilarious spots. But for a poem whose only conceivable subject is the accomplishments of its own completion, this is a real success. And its final success can be found in the remainder of Koch's poetry, wherein the parable of *Ko*'s quest for completion is played out in a variety of ways.

As I mentioned earlier, I miss some favorite poems here ("The Young Park," "The Scales," "The Interpretation of Dreams"—all from *The Pleasures of Peace*). But his volume includes almost all of the poems in *Thank You,* and all of them in the splendid recent volume, *The Art of Love,* whose title poem forms an Ovidian, didactic tetrad with three others ("Some General Instructions," "The Art of Poetry," "On Beauty"). Their late manner is more that of a teacher than of an eternal ephebe—one may compare the *Duck Soup*–like mise-en-scène of the poet's early "Fresh Air" with his more recent ars poetica, just as he himself invites you to look back at the early "The Circus" through (or is it past? over? under? around?) the later poem, which purports to try to remember the occasions on which the first was composed. In these poems, the wild turns of the earlier ones are there in smaller scale, and the parody of the didactic mode enables a literal one to work under the disguise of its own caricature. The shift in successive strophes toward the end of "The Art of Love" from the stand-up comic through the mellowed air of practical wisdom on the realm of the powers for which all poetry longs may be seen in

> Zombie-itis is love of the living dead. It is comparatively rare.
> If a woman likes it, you can probably find other things she likes
>   that you will like even more.
>
> Ten things an older man must never say to a younger woman:
> 1) I'm dying! 2) I can't hear what you're saying! 3) How many
>   fingers are you holding up?

4) Listen to my heart. 5) Take my pulse. 6) What's your name?
7) Is it cold in here? 8) Is it hot in here? 9) Are you in here?
10) What wings are those beating at the window?
Not that a man should stress his youth in a dishonest way
But that he should not unduly emphasize his age.

The inability to love is almost incurable. A long sea voyage
Is recommended, in the company of an irresistible girl.

To turn a woman into a duck, etc., hypnotize her and dress her
    in a costume.
To make love standing in water, see "Elephant Congress" in the
    Kama Sutra (chap. iv).
During a shortage of girls, visit numerous places; give public
    lectures; carry this volume.

—where "a duck, etc.," is absolutely masterful. These poems, and "Days and Nights" and the very moving "With Janice" are marked by an imaginative maturity always wanting to brood on its own childhood, and never failing to startle us in old-new-old ways.

W. H. Auden

A First Encounter

I am reticent about writing of my first meeting with W. H. Auden because of my own peculiarly bad memory for things said on particular occasions, and, more interestingly, because of some of his own implicit injunctions. I can almost hear him propounding them in his characteristic mode of semiprivate declamation: (1) There should be no gossip in or for print and (2) when you write of something or someone don't talk about yourself. On an occasion like this I could only wish to be—"an idiot with total recall." Not having anything like that kind of recall, it is hard to stay invisible. Besides, I was then at such an awkward age—not yet eighteen and an uneducated sophomore in college—that I was totally unable to ask him the questions that, on so many occasions since, I have wished I could have put to him as he was then (at the age of forty, seventeen years younger than I am now). And yet Auden was the poet whose cadences had become so much an undersong in my own verse that, ten years after that first meeting, I still had to rewrite in proof many lines of my first book of poems, to expunge embarrassingly blatant echoes of his voice.

That "voice" is a trope in disfavor in fashionably advanced academic critical circles today is of little matter for serious poetry. Before I ever met him, I had (as Hazlitt put it) "a sound in my ears—it was the voice of Fancy; I had a light before me—it was the face of Poetry." The sound had come from the pages of

---

This was one of a set of brief, commissioned memoirs by various hands, relating memorable encounters with celebrated people no longer alive. From *Yale Review*, 77, no. 4 (summer 1988); later reprinted in Kai Erikson, ed., *Encounters* (Yale University Press, 1989).

Auden's poetry: in my freshman year at Columbia I had bought a copy of the 1945 *Collected Poems*, still in its dark-green binding—a slimmer volume than subsequent printings produced because of the thin, gray wartime paper. In the first semester of my freshman year I remember thinking of Robinson Jeffers as a favorite contemporary poet, but during the remainder of that year I began to read Auden, Yeats, and Stevens, puzzling them out by myself. And while I had committed to memory more lines of Eliot, Pound, and these three other poets than I had of Keats, Shelley, or Wordsworth, it was Auden's *voice* that I fancied I heard coming off the page at me.

The poems I knew best then were an odd assortment of light pieces and portions of *The Sea and the Mirror*. But there were others, too, including "Heavy Date," "O, Where Are You Going?" "Musée des Beaux-Arts," and "September 1, 1939," of course, with its figure of contingent hope, the "ironic points of light"—which spoke at once to my New Yorker's native landscape and my moviegoer's familiarity with its black-and-white transformations in night background shots. (Eventually Auden repudiated "September 1, 1939." "I won't let you reprint it," he said to me years later, "because, you know, it's bogus.") Then, too, there were poems like "The Maze" and "Law Like Love," the ballads, and the elegies for Freud and Yeats—all these spoke to me in the imagined tones of the voice of a teacher. My only other teacher-at-a-distance had been George Bernard Shaw, whom I had started reading in elementary school. Shaw, Auden, and, later on, Orwell all served at various times as moral teachers for me, but Auden was the only one I ever knew. On first meeting him I seem now to have heard his imagined voice and his actual one, which I came to know so well in later years, blended indefinably.

The increasingly famous Face was another matter. Before reading a word of him, I remember seeing his photograph accompanying a lead review of the *Collected Poems* in either the *New York Times Book Review* or the *Saturday Review of Literature*. I first read then, in 1945, about this important younger poet. I had heard his name before only in some joking light verse (by Morris Bishop, I believe, with a dreadful pun that delighted me at fourteen, something about "Whether we ought or whether we Auden"), but when I asked for an explanation I was told only that his was the name of a clever modern poet. I am shocked now by the actual pictures of him taken in those years, partially because my memory is primarily of that later Face ("He's been years building it up," a common friend said years later), with its remarkable systems of wrinkles, palimpsestically overlaid on what I saw but cannot now actually remember.

In any event, my first glimpses of the poet himself had been prepared for by a good deal of adulation, and somewhat less knowledge, of the man and the work. I had known that he was then living at 7 Cornelia Street, a stone's throw from the building in Greenwich Village that housed the printers of the *Columbia Spectator,* for which I had written a good deal of news and feature copy as a freshman, and which I frequently had to put to bed downtown late at night. (The abode of e. e. cummings on Patchin Place was also known to me and some friends, and occasionally haunted for ten minutes or so in the hopes of catching a Glimpse.) But I had never seen or heard Auden, even publicly, until the late winter of 1947, when I was in my second year at Columbia.

He was then appearing at Barnard College to teach a course under Ursula Niebuhr's auspices called "The Quest in Ancient and Modern Literature." A young lady I was pursuing at the time was taking it, and various Quests of my own—for the poet's voice and face, for a sip of Castalian water, for the lady's company and (I hoped) person—all converged on the lecture room. I attended a few of those sessions, daunted by the reading list (from *Gilgamesh*—this was the first I had heard of it— through Kafka's *The Castle*) and fascinated by the originality of the agenda. I had loved since childhood "The Hunting of the Snark" and Edward Lear's "The Jumblies," but to hear this somewhat high-pitched and unresonant voice bracketing these with *Moby-Dick* in a mode of romantic Argonautica was electrifying. (Some of his observations would resurface later on in the lectures he gave at the University of Virginia, which became that unique and wonderful little book called *The Enchafèd Flood.*) But not being officially enrolled in the course, I was far too shy to approach the speaker after class.

The first occasion at which we actually met was on an evening in May of that year, at a dinner celebrating the annual Boar's Head Poetry Prizes at Columbia, newly instituted after World

War II. Columbia undergraduates competed for first and second prizes of one hundred dollars and fifty dollars, if I remember correctly (a considerable sum in those days—thirty dollars was a month's rent in a comfortable, safe, Lower East Side cold-water flat). The money came from funds given to the then-moribund literary society called Philoexian; it originally endowed a grand prize for a patriotic oration, to consist of a plaster cast of Houdon's bust of George Washington, with its huge jaws. The *Columbia Review* sought to use these funds for a poetry contest that had been held before the war, accompanied by a reading and an Honored Guest. Due to the efforts of the business manager, a nascent lawyer, we contrived to have the income of the patriotic bust fund diverted to the service of Calliope. (I must add that, a very few years later, the contest for the patriotic oration was gravely and frivolously reintroduced for a year, the prize being won with a ringing encomium of Henry James's essay on Hawthorne—what could be more *American?*—by the precociously sophisticated Robert Gottlieb.) There were sufficiently few contestants in 1947 (in those decent days of *poeta fit, non nascitur,* fewer young persons believed themselves to be bards than do today's multitudes) to allow for all of them to read one or two poems after the prizewinners had been celebrated and the Honored Guest heard from.

His presence on Morningside Heights earlier that spring allowed us to think of asking Auden, and, to our delight, he agreed to come uptown and to sing for what was only his supper (he asked to read through the student poems and to make a few comments at the reading). As the precocious but naive editor of the *Columbia Review* that year (the unstaffed but college-funded quarterly had fallen to me, a sophomore, by default), I got to plan the evening, arrange the dinner at the Faculty Club, and attend it ex officio, for my wretched poems had not placed at all in the competition. The prizewinners were a returned World War II pilot named Coman Leavenworth, who had written some amazingly polished and (I now see) very Audenesque poems, and Allen Ginsberg, whose entry was a pastiche of Marvell's "The Garden." They, the editors, and the judges of the contest—that year they were Lionel Trilling and the formidable and locally fabulous Andrew Chiappe—assembled for dinner, before the reading, with Auden.

I waited for him by the door. I noticed that he was wearing carpet slippers and felt there to be something peculiar about this: were his feet bad? or temporarily injured? or had he forgotten his shoes in a rush to get here on time? Two summers before, when working as an office boy at the *New Yorker,* I had had to pick up some proofs from the celebrated cartoonist Peter Arno at his Park Avenue apartment at two in the afternoon: he came to the door in pajamas and dressing gown, which seemed marvelously louche to me at the time, and there was *something* about those carpet slippers. There was also something resonant about his first words after the perfunctory greetings. In response to a waiter who appeared with a request for a drink order, he said—and I can still hear the sound of his voice, though I can scarcely remember what he sounded like in those lectures at Barnard—"I'll have an old-fashioned, please." Of this, too, I wondered at the possible significance (barely of drinking age, I had only a visionary taxonomy of mixed drinks). Was there something about this choice of drink that I didn't know? Was its name self-descriptive of its social style? Or was it preferred in the literary circles, mysteriously both advanced and established, in which I supposed the poet to move?

Of the early dinner (in those days the Columbia Faculty Club was not noted for its cuisine, although for a shy sophomore it was a low-voltage thrill to be eating there at all), I can remember nothing, and of the discourse, very little. Considering the conversation of other guests and what they must have said, this vacancy of memory is all a bit shocking and, to me, now, terribly disappointing. It was in all innocence that, in my youth, I could never keep a journal—it seemed too self-important, and was indeed too demanding of a consistency of attention I didn't possess. And so I was rather like a child being taken to see various wonders of a minor world—the gardens of Castle Rubbish, the Great Memorial Museum, the cute-as-a-button one-ring circus—and remembering not the famous and canonical sights but only the train ride, the pattern of tiles on the floor of the men's room, the discovered delights of a complex of interconnected rooms, things no grown-up would notice. So with the old-fashioned, and the sound of the voice. I was lost in an inner museum of my own, trying to put together the particular cadences, the variations of pitch, the speeding up and slowing down of the phrases in conversation that sounded so different from the imperfectly enunciated and sometimes swallowed reading of his Barnard lectures (James Merrill conjures these up marvelously on the pages of *The Changing Light at Sandover*) with the fictive inner voice I had heard speaking his poems to me from the page. But it was the sound of that voice—its famously wide range of pitch, its periodic slowing of articulation, its bursts of speed at what even then were homiletic moments (and here the speaker became a strange combination of tutor, nanny, and coconspirator)—that marked his speech, even as the "we" of many of his poems compounded the usage of the editorial desk, the royal proclamation, the pulpit, and the nursery.

I do remember his talking at the reading of the importance of young poets' using models well to discover their own voices, and, as always, of the significance of form. The audience in the well-filled room wanted, I think, to hear more from him about crisis theology and Marxism, about "private faces in public places"—as he put it in the epigraph to *The Orators*—and about the relation of criticism to poetry. Allen Ginsberg, who had written a brief essay on *The Sea and the Mirror* for our magazine the previous spring, was concerned with that poem in particular; but what fascinated me was the introduction Auden gave to the value of difficulty—not in construing but in constructing, in "making," to invoke his own later triad, rather than merely in knowing and judging. He may have invoked Paul Valéry then, as I know he did in a conversation fourteen years later: "I agree with Valéry when he says a poet is a person whose imagination is stimulated by arbitrary rules. He meant that if it is not stimulated but is insulted by them, he'd better write prose." But I had been bottle-fed (by the magical attentions of Brooks and Warren's textbook, *Understanding Poetry*, which I had read while in high school) on the notion of formal strictures holding in check passionate thoughts and cognitively charged passions, and this other notion filled me with some wonder.

I think, too, that this was the first occasion on which I heard him talk of the elements of problem-solving and of unriddling that poetry and crossword puzzles have in common. It was certainly the scene of my being introduced to the idea that playing with words, loving them and their apparent relations, characters, and habits, was more essential to the birth of poetry than lofty thoughts, aesthetic programs (particularly radically modernist ones), or even being enamored of Eros—and enamored I was at that time. (Not yet eighteen, yet spiritually fuzzy around the edges, I described myself—recording my grim joke in a notebook—as "Half in death with easeful love.") I couldn't easily believe that the Muse was made of language rather than of a particular absent body, and could be a stern monitor of one's behavior in times of intellectual crisis (which I had heard about in relation to Auden, but didn't know enough about modern theology even to grasp weakly). But coming over the years to understand how and in what ways this was true has been an important side road on the map of my life as a writer, and wonder at the notion started that evening. Fourteen years later, in 1961, in the visionary clutter of the St. Mark's Place apartment that was his last dwelling in New York City, he summed this matter up resonantly, fully of overtones of Lichtenberg, Karl Kraus, and some of his other favorite aphorists: "A poet is someone who uses a language he didn't create, which has its own wonderful property. And one is in the position—rather of, well—it's like a marriage bed where the poet speaks as the husband and the language is the wife who bears the child. And naturally, she has a lot to say in what is said." (I can record this, not from an incredible lapse of my usual amnesia, but from notes taken at the time for a *Paris Review* interview that never crystallized.)

I can also remember that he mentioned, in a brief discussion that followed the reading and his public remarks, that he had been working on a new poem (I now estimate that it had been finished some time in February). He talked primarily of its formal mode of alliterative verse, with which I was slightly familiar from having read parts of *Piers Plowman* for a survey course in English literature. That new poem was *The Age of Anxiety,* which I got to read when it was published that summer. It happened that I was in Denver on my way across the country, staying briefly with Allen Ginsberg, who told me of the poem's appearance; I went with him to a bookstore and bought a copy (it's inscribed "July 10, 1947"). We sat outdoors and read parts of it aloud, and I remember Allen maintaining that the "lost dad, / Our colossal father" in the section called "The Dirge" must be Roosevelt. Be that as may be, I cannot remember Wystan Auden saying anything much to me on that night in May, nor, indeed, a few weeks later when he also came to Columbia to read "Music Is International" as the Phi Beta Kappa poem that year.

In fact, I would not see him again for five years—five years during which I got to know most of his work rather well, had his companion Chester Kallman pointed out to me at the San Remo bar, became acquainted with his friend Alan Ansen, read "In Praise of Limestone" in *Horizon*, graduated from college, went abroad, and returned to graduate school at Indiana University. In Bloomington, in the winter of 1952–53, I finally got to meet and talk with him. He had given a well-attended reading in a rather grand hall and was staying the night at the student union building, a totally dry establishment on a totally dry campus. This time I did go backstage, blessed with a bit more assurance, and, presuming on the occasion he must have forgotten and on the name of a common acquaintance or two, I secured a meeting at breakfast the next morning, in a large student cafeteria with jukeboxes going even at that time of day. He complained of being given fruit punch the night before, and I had to explain the unavailability of liquor. But he talked of many things during that hour and a half, and by then I knew much more of what he, I myself, and the matter of poetry all were, so that the occasion was less awesome but far more satisfactory than my first meeting with him had been.

This was the first time at which he said certain things that he would reiterate over the years that I knew him. On hearing that I was studying for a Ph.D. and working in the Renaissance, he made it clear that he disapproved of teaching "creative writing." Praising colleges and universities as patrons of writers, he insisted that the writers should not agree to have anything to do with teaching contemporary literature. "They should teach the eighteenth century or something," he said. Years later he would confess that even in teaching a historical body of literature, he would prefer not to assign papers to the students, but rather have them write stylistic pastiches of the poems, plays, or novels in question, arguing that such would constitute a far better test of what they had been able to apprehend. I don't know if he ever actually did this, however. Questions of poetry and science came up, and he was interested to learn that my father was a physiologist, remarking that his father had been a doctor and that he had grown up in a house where—as he put it some years later, I remember—"science and literature were both humanities." When in 1962 he did meet my father at a party, he spent a good deal of time talking with him, and would inquire about him subsequently. And in the days, a few years after, when my father was dying, I found that Wystan Auden was the one person I could talk to of my agitation about medical and familial pretense and euphemism: he told me then of how he had been able to discuss his own father's dying with him, as I had not been able to do.

He also spoke then of the upcoming first performance at the Metropolitan Opera of *The Rake's Progress,* two and a half years after its world premiere in Venice, and of how he preferred singers to American actors for speaking verse in the theater. I remember very well his lack of interest in talking about his early plays, and his extremely resonant remark about the difference between writing for composers and for silent readers, as poets today usually do. "The success in writing for music," he said, "consists in how well what you write will get the composer to compose." This led to matters of poetic impersonality more generally, and his saying that he thought poets ought, particularly when young, to look like everyone else—something that, I did not add at the time, I had, unhappily, always failed to do. I was just beginning to understand in those days how the rhetoric of personal distancing that was so personal a matter for T. S. Eliot had become something of a modernist principle. But in any case, these were the days of America's introduction to the elaborately rhapsodic public performances of Dylan Thomas, and his cautioning against the public role of the *poète maudit* thus had more than antiquarian interest.

I could never, in those days, think of myself as a poet (nor, indeed, would I allow myself to, or to accept the word as designation, until I was thirty-five and had published three books of poems). If one was serious, one had the good sense and taste not to make such a claim. But I had recently published three prose poems in something grander than a campus journal—the *New Directions* annual, which also contained prose poems by my slightly older contemporaries Allen Ginsberg and John Ashbery (Ashbery's were the good ones)—which may have helped me in some part to begin to entertain the possibility, during this conversation, of my having some future literary legitimacy. But perhaps it was only the fact of the informality of the breakfast. (How much less alarming now were the carpet slippers in which he again appeared!) I was the kind of fan, I fear, that I would myself today pray silently for the patience to deal with; Auden's generosity with his time was nothing I could understand then. Nor could I begin to conceive of how I was more deeply and mysteriously affected by these early encounters with Auden than with later ones that might at first appear to be more significant: my correspondence with him over his having taken my first book of verse for the Yale Series of Younger Poets (because I so deeply admired some of his previous selections, this was particularly moving for me); the occasion, beautifully arranged by our common friend William Meredith, at which I was reintroduced, somewhat more *au pair,* after my book had appeared; and all the other occasions over the subsequent years, the meetings in New York, New Haven (where I then taught), New York again.

Only the very last time I saw Auden, visiting him and Chester Kallman in Kirchstetten with my wife and young daughters, on the way to spend a week in Vienna, is now as resonant. Even in that last, somewhat ill, somewhat cranky stage of his life his generosity toward my children is memorable. He asked all in the room—and them particularly—to try to recall the earliest public event they remembered, mentioning that in his case it was hearing of the *Titanic* disaster. (For my older daughter, it was John Kennedy's assassination; for her sister, four years younger, it was the murder of his brother; for me, it was actually seeing the *Morro Castle* burning off the New Jersey shore.) It was a sunny July day; we arrived by car, amused and delighted to see that the street he lived on, Hinterholz, had been renamed Audenstrasse. He had recently returned from reading at a Poetry International Festival in London, where he had had an amusing and slightly awkward encounter with Allen Ginsberg; his mentioning this caused me to remind him of the original occasion at the Boar's Head Poetry Reading when we had first met, and, indeed, of the importance of his presence in New York during the following fifteen years for so many poets of my generation— not just to those of us who had been at Columbia, including Richard Howard, Daniel Hoffman, and Louis Simpson, but James Merrill and John Ashbery as well. I had, of course, not the slightest notion that I would never see him again, that he would die two months later, at the same age as my father.

A short time ago, I called my daughter, who is now a graduate student in California, to talk about the occasion. I asked her what she particularly remembered. She said it was a picture of Yeats on the wall, which she recognized, and Chester Kallman's splendid lunch, at which she had encountered polenta for the first time. This was her "I'll have an old-fashioned, please." It was a far more emblematic token than mine.

IV

Something of Myself

Working through Poems

An Interview by Langdon Hammer

John, a sentence from one of your classes has stayed on my mind for probably fifteen years now. That sentence is: "Poems get to be about the world by being about how to talk about it." Help me understand that.

It amuses me to hear you quote me from back then. What I was saying was ad hoc to a polarized debate between deconstructive theorists on the one hand, who would hate the notion that any text is about anything, and on the other hand, terribly literal-minded critics who would say that a poem is about a subject as if it were an essay or scientific paper or historical paper or a piece of polemic. I wished to talk about the complicated dialectic between these two points of view. One way a poem gets to be about things—about things in the world, about human experience, about human experience's ability to contemplate itself (those things that distinguish us from even what we feel now to be the more sentient beasts)—is by looking inward. Poetry is a use of language in which language is opaque rather than transparent, and in which what is being said about the world immediately becomes part of the world as it comes to be uttered; so the misuses of language, the games played with language, are all part of the essential work of what poetry does. I put this rather dramatically because I knew undergraduates would have heard the notion that poetry can be only about itself, as if it were chess; and they might also have heard a stonewalling objection to that on the grounds that there is no problem about meaning or

From *Southwest Review* 80 (fall 1995); this interview with my colleague and former student was conducted in the fall of 1993.

reference. Neither of these views is true; they are like the head and tail of the same false coin.

One thing I like about that formulation is the series of three abouts, *which makes it hard to say. It's as if you were saying, poems can and must pass out of literature into life, but they can only get there by roundabout and arduous routes, entailing discipline and seriousness. Which makes me think that writing poems poses, in your view, a specifically ethical challenge. I wonder what kinds of ethical work are entailed in the writing of poetry. I also wonder what the ethics of writing have to do with the observance of rules.*

That's a wonderful question, and I suppose simply to start answering it would be the beginning of a long book. Let me take the easier part first, which is the whole question of rules. The heroic, romantic story holds that there was a rule book and hacks wrote by it, until X the Genius came along, threw the rules away, and did great things. That's not the way it goes. The question is (*a*) *which* rules? and (*b*) how were they being followed to begin with? You do set rules for yourself that have some relation to rules other people have set, but the setting of those rules for yourself involves reconfiguration and creation as well as acknowledgment. Then there is the question of how you respond to the rules you set yourself. One of the ways to define a bad or inept writer is a writer who has set up certain rules and then not followed them, as if they weren't rules. One needs to know what a rule is—what it governs, what it doesn't. Now, when one writes something that deliberately purports to follow certain rules, and then one breaks a rule at a certain point, the breakage of the rule is a very important move, and it has to carry weight and be justified. It can be significant or it can be trivial. For example, somebody writes a sonnet and then, talking about some phenomenon in the middle of the sonnet, wants to observe that there is something else opposed to this intricate phenomenon, which is very small and trivial; and he so constitutes the sixth line of the sonnet that it designates that thing in a line that is only four syllables long. You might say the rule is broken, and there's justification for it, but that breaking and that justification are splendid only on a kindergarten level.

Now, I wouldn't insist that this discourse about rules (which you could then go into in incredible detail, discussing formal rules, rules of diction, all the ground rules of the speech game) necessarily involves ethical questions, rather than purely epistemological ones. When it comes to the ethics of writing poems, I think of a line of Auden's from "In Praise of Limestone" that I remember from college: "or ruin a fine tenor voice / For effects that bring down the house." This is a fundamental notion about what makes art different from public performance, theater, showbiz, etc.: cheap shots aimed to bring down the house are simply bad news and the enemy of art. On reflection, I'd have to say I don't know whether not knowing that a rhetorical or stylistic move is too easy, or an effect too glitzy, is worse than the other case—knowing it is and not caring. George Herbert's "Decking the sense as if it were to sell," or doing the decking not knowing you're doing it, or that there is any sense at all, or whatever. There are ample places for both of those conditions to perform in. True poetry is not one of those.

Give me an example of a "cheap shot."

A low-grade cheap shot might be a gross or lurid sentimentality, a gratuitous shocker, an appeal to fashion without acknowledgment that it was that, and so forth. A higher-grade one might be the end of Oscar Wilde's "The Harlot's House" where, in place of narrative or interpretive resolution, he offers, "Down the long and silent street, / The dawn, with silver-sandalled feet, / Crept like a frightened girl." Wilde—one of the great teachers of this moral lesson—should certainly have known better.

When you mentioned Auden a few moments ago, I was reminded of Vision and Resonance, *where you refer to Auden's ear for prosody as "something like a moral sense." What kind of moral sense exactly?*

Well, it's simply that Auden's ear heard faults as if they were sins, if one can imagine the notion of a sin against the *logos,* using *the logos* totally in a secular sense. If you don't care about the language, and language isn't terribly, terribly important for you, then the way in which you misuse it or trash it doesn't matter.

All right. Now I want to bring some of these questions to your own poetry. When you read your Selected Poetry, *a selection from four decades of writing, I wonder what sort of plot you see in that book, what kind of story?*

Looking at the early work just turns me to stone. It's not really that good. When I say "that good," I mean I wish I could have started writing with my third book. It's a little bit as if my work had grown up in a foster home. And I had—without making a legal case about it, or complaining that I had been wounded by reality—managed to discover as a result of wandering out of home that I really was at home somewhere else, and could come back to that true home. But it didn't happen with any conversion experience or moment of fanfare.

What was that foster home?

It was the poetic climate that I started writing in. There was wonderful tutelage: some of it came from Auden, some of it came from John Crowe Ransom, some of it from a New Critical agenda. There was an emphasis on technique, and on what constituted putting something right. At this point I really couldn't read Whitman very well. I couldn't even read Milton very well. When I was in high school, I read some Pound, was puzzled by it, but entranced. Gertrude Stein remarked that Pound was the village explainer, great if you were a village, if not, not. Yet I think a lot of young American poets of my generation *were* villages, and Pound was a great explainer for us. When we stopped being villages, he stopped being a great explainer, and that's all right.

Was there a specific turning point?

Well, the poem called "The Night Mirror." It was the first time I'd ever written something that I could say—and this isn't an attempt to be paradoxical or puzzling—I didn't understand. It *was* a poem, and I knew that everything had to be there in it, but I didn't quite know why I'd written it and I didn't quite know what it added up to, even when I made it the title poem of *The Night Mirror*. I didn't really know what the phrase meant, but there it was. It literally was a mirror that a child wakes up looking at in a room at night, so it was the mirror at night. But it was also "nightmare" and a hundred other things; it was a very over-determined poem. Interestingly enough, it had in it the report of a dream of mine, the trace of a childhood dream. I'd never included an actual dream in a poem before.

You must mean the grandmother's "blood-red" face.

Yes, a bit of nightmare, one of the earliest nightmares I had. My closest poetic friend and severest critic at the time read it and pronounced it of all the poems—and I liked all the other poems in the book much better—he pronounced it very different from the others.

I want to understand this turning point better. Among your peers, and I'm thinking of poets as different from you and from each other as Merwin and Rich, there are dramatic moments of transformation, in which the poet has broken with or away from earlier styles and attitudes and manners. That wouldn't, on the surface at any rate, seem to be the case with your work.

There'd been a break, but not on the level of style. The break was very deep. Let me explain it this way. When I started to write, there were several attempts to politicize formal things: if you weren't writing free verse, you were called "academic" by writers who were themselves so academic they piously spelled *should* and *would* sh/d and w/d, as Pound had done in his letters fifty years earlier. This was the time of Donald Allen's anthology for Grove Press, about 1960, the book calling itself *The New American Poets,* and another volume, the one in which some of my work appeared, *The New Poets of England and America.* (Both of these titles use the definite article, which I would never use in an anthology, because it's always not "the," but *some.*) We were choosing up sides in the sandlot. And I felt that there were guys on my team who weren't on my side, and there were guys on the other team who *were* on my side. So I began to realize that whoever had chosen up sides on the basis of formal style didn't know anything about poetry. But my own sense of where I was had to struggle against all these false constructions of where I was. It was an important lesson—that what makes a poet is not style alone, but something far deeper.

I want to know about that deeper thing. Tell me how you think your poetry has changed, or how it's changed and stayed the same, over the years.

Well, I still like to make jokes, but I think the jokes are in the service of something else, and they're much more grim. And they're also, I hope, sitting over, and concerned with, deeper problems. Maybe it's a result of coming to terms with certain kinds of philosophical impulse that I think I've always had, but they were much more narrow. It's as if some of the way some of the poems talk had been locked into the analytic, philosophical discourse of, say, the 1950s, my early infatuation with which I have since outgrown, because I am interested in terrible questions. But it seems to me that the natural world of language is so full of wonders that even in the pursuit of the terrible questions these things come up. The trouble is, I think, that there are still people who, when they want to praise my work, say, oh, it's witty, without seeing anything else about it. I believe that they haven't read it, because that is not certainly the point, and I've written a lot of very, very sad poetry.

"Terrible questions"—which questions exactly?

Well, I suppose what Freud called—in *The Future of an Illusion,* I think—"the troublesome riddle of death." Certainly one kind of philosopher writes as though he or she thinks of death as the condition in which questions can't be asked or answered, and thus not very interesting. Another kind might write as if nothing else were really interesting. Or, at best, as if death shaped the very notion of what questioning and answering were. I suppose that I feel like one kind of writer at noon, and another at midnight; but as a poet, I have to sing of the whole day, with all the contrarieties it contains.

You do *"sing of the whole day" in your poetry—by which I mean you've written "very sad" poems, as you say, but also, well, happy poems, exuberant and amusing poems. In fact, it seems to me that sadness isn't something opposed to your wittiness, something set apart from it. Your funniest poetry (and you're one of a small number of poets who do write funny poems, who take humor seriously, so to speak)—your funniest poetry is also full of sadness.*

I've never felt that *funny* and *serious* were opposites: the opposition is *funny/solemn* and *frivolous/serious*. Much solemnity is a costume for what is deeply frivolous (and, for example, someone with no sense of humor had better be astonishingly brilliant not to be frivolous, as all dullness is). Sadness, though: perhaps I dwell a lot on losses, and, being a bad domestic economist, often can't perceive the gains, at least until too late. And that's additionally a bit sad. And about wit—I think it's always a question of what the wit is directed *at*. Since I love language and I'm amused by dwelling in a state of both *having* and *getting* to use it, language and this aspect of it frequently become—they both become—the target for me of its most polished resources.

A moment ago you spoke of "the natural world of language." You called it a world of "wonders"—something that distracts you even in the pursuit of "terrible questions." What did you mean?

It's just that I notice things about language—my own, those of others, systems of signs that are like and unlike natural languages—the way I notice things about the rest of nature. This is part of what comes up in a very short recent poem of mine—it may be a fragment, it may be an aphorism, it may end up being part of something longer, I don't know. It's called, at this stage, "Semiology":

> The warning amber drains the going green
> Of hope, and points toward the arresting red
> Which strangely—given what we've made it mean—
>   Rhymes with *Go Ahead!*
>
> A glint of hopeful color in the pigments
> Of our red signals is itself a sign:
> The frightful hard *g* in the word *malignant*'s
>   Silent in *benign.*

I suppose if there's any true poetry here, it probably resides in the *relation* between the two stanzas—not just the paradoxes of apparent contradiction, but something more. For example, that *g* is also silent in *sign*—a central term here—and what to make of that, is part of the poem, although not loudly displayed. But the whole argument could be seen as moving only toward the bottom line, as it were, of the closing, in which case it would be taken merely as what in German is called *Galgenhumor*, gallows humor.

Now that we're talking about the philosophical dimensions of your work, I want to ask you about the poem "Tesserae" and the beautiful quatrain that begins the last section:

> *These lines, these bits and pieces, each a token*
> *Of ruined method, of "a knowledge broken,"*
> *Inaudible, leave traces when they pass*
> *As if the fragments of our speech had spoken.*

"Tesserae" is made up of 144 quatrains, almost any one of which could have stood by itself as a short, independent poem. What is the "ruined method" of which those many quatrains are the tokens?

I'm not sure I know, that is, I know the quatrain and I'm not sure how to paraphrase it. Strange, because I've always felt that paraphrasability was crucial. But I suppose I now write a lot of poems, that, like "The Night Mirror," I can't understand, which is why I think they may be better. I'll try to deal with some of what I had in mind here. The "knowledge broken" is from Bacon. I lost the place I had got it from; it was in a book, and I'd underlined it. "A knowledge broken": the grammar is funny and it would have to be seventeenth-century, meaning a way of knowledge, a method of knowledge, a good knowledge—it's so broken, and I loved all that in that broken fragment of phrase. Also, that is one of the quatrains in which I was very consciously meditating on what the hell I do. What am I doing writing these little bits and pieces? Who do I think I am doing this? Is it being afraid to write a huge long thing? What of huge long things in general? The huge long thing of mine I'd been most pleased with was "Powers of Thirteen"; that poem was fragmentary, but at least each unit was like the others, being a funny version of a sonnet, each consisting of thirteen lines of thirteen syllables. It is my major sonnet sequence, and they're not really sonnets. "Tesserae" is a kind of echo in the aftermath of that, broken off from it. The quatrains in it are all epigrams. I've always felt the epigram was getting at truth rather like a hit-and-run driver, as opposed to a responsible driver who hits truth and then stays around laboriously to pick up the pieces, which is what I consider philosophy to be. So the knowledge I speak of in the quatrain you quoted is a poetic knowledge broken off from a large structure—I wrote it in bits and pieces after all—at the same time that these bits and pieces were fragments of something else. And that last line: "As if the fragments of our speech had spoken," it just grew out of the lines before; it is the thing that pulls it all together, even though I'm not quite sure what it means yet.

It interests me that a poet so concerned with knowledge—with the poetic terms in which it can be gained—values his poems most when he can't understand them. You'll have to explain what you mean when you say you don't understand a poem you wrote!

I talked about this earlier, in connection with "The Night Mirror." I could usually tell you why in any poem I'd done what I'd done, at almost any level, from title and scale and scope and formal frame down to minutiae of diction and word placement. In that poem, I couldn't at all—I just knew that everything there had to be there the way it was. I've only gradually come to understand some of what the poem was "about"—the way in which dreams *are* poems, and the way thinking about them darkens the whole question of artistic intention, among other things. I felt that the poem was writing itself, using me as I might use a pen or a typewriter. But I can only get at fragments of all that . . .

It seems to me that, especially in "Tesserae," you are less interested in wholes than in fragments.

The whole question of fragmentariness is something I thought about a lot before "Tesserae" in the course of writing that very difficult poem "Harp Lake." One thing about "Tesserae" is, it's not difficult. What's very problematic is how it's put together and what it adds up to. "Harp Lake" is very difficult partially because I was responding to a tradition of difficulty I'd not much dealt with. The poet that most lay behind "Harp Lake" was René Char. Char had always seemed to me in his short poems to juxtapose two utterances and say that the basis of the implied simile lay in the fact that he had juxtaposed them. And I was interested in the formal device of the Malay pantoum, which I had learned about from two friends of mine who both know Malay very well and who had lived there for a long time—they were married, one of them an anthropologist, one a painter. They had talked to me about real *pantun,* as opposed to the French *pantoum,* and had shown me some, and I'd then gotten a little book called *Teach Yourself Malay* and a Malay grammar. I was fascinated by the delicate relation between the first and the second part of these Malay epigrams. In the sample one I wrote, punning on "pontoons"—

—you mean, "The Catamaran," included in Harp Lake:

> *Pantuns in the original Malay*
> *Are quatrains of two thoughts, but of one mind.*
> *Athwart these two pontoons I sail away,*
> *Yet touching neither; land lies far behind.*

Yes. There, in "The Catamaran," I tried to explain the relation between the two parts. And once I had worked through all that, the voice of those other quatrains, namely the Fitzgerald version of *The Rubaiyat of Omar Khayyam,* which I've known since childhood, started coming back to haunt me, and "Tesserae" got started.

Describe the relation between the pantoum and the Rubaiyat quatrain.

The Rubaiyat quatrain is not going to puzzle in the relation of its two parts. It's open to any one of a number of moves. You have four lines, the third one nonrhyming and the fourth one bringing it back into the rhyme again. You can still go "A, A, A but B." You can break it into two parts. You can have it one long utterance. You can string a long periodic sentence through it.

You can break it up into bits. You can, and I could not resist the temptation of doing so in one case, bury another rhyme form within it (the way I'd done in a much larger way in "Powers of Thirteen"). I played with all these options, and treated it as if this were the only way I could talk. And it *was* the only way I could poetically talk for a long time. After I had written a few of them, I wanted to see what they looked like in print, so I had to gather some together: there were ad hoc seasonal groupings—for example, that summer one that appeared in the *New Yorker*. It was like having a box of beads that you've made carefully and somebody wants to see them, so you say OK, I'll take some and string them together to show others, and then you take them off the string and put them in the box again. That's what happened with that poem. The brilliant suggestion to break it up through the book into four sections was that of my editor, the noble and wonderful Harry Ford. An absolutely remarkable man, by the way, one of the few people still in publishing who is vastly knowledgeable, a great aesthete, and a great designer. It was Harry Ford's suggestion to break the poem up—

—into four sections?

Well, he didn't say exactly how many sections. He said break it up in more than two. And four sections gave me the right structure. There's no "plot" as such, except for a vague seasonal drift and a mapping of ancient temperamental patterns on that drift.

About the title.

Oh, very good. I didn't know what the hell I was going to call it. It just came to me one day that that's what they were—that is, "tesserae" because they were like tiles of a mosaic, yet they were also tesserae because they were four-sided, rectangular tiles for a mosaic, also simply quatrains. The issue of the fourness of them, it had to be that.

One place I've seen the word is in The Anxiety of Influence, *where it's the name of one of Bloom's revisionary ratios.*

That's right. I had forgotten that totally. Now let's see, which one is it?

It has to do with the way a poet "completes" a precursor. Tesserae *in that context refers to the broken pieces of pottery that, when joined together, were used by members of a mystery cult to recognize each other.*

As when in low-grade espionage you tear up a dollar bill in a certain way and leave the other person the other half of the bill and that's his contact. Well, what can I say? Perhaps I had repressed that, or perhaps Bloom's use of the word and mine come from the same place.

How important to the poem was the source of its quatrains in Fitzgerald?

I grew up knowing *The Rubaiyat.* My mother had an edition with at least four different versions of the translation and Edmund Dulac's illustrations, and I had those things in my head. Anybody who'd been to school knew a few of them: "A book of verses underneath the bough, / A loaf of bread, a jug of wine and thou / Beside me singing in the wilderness, / Ah wilderness were paradise enow"—so that Eugene O'Neill could use "Ah Wilderness" as the title of a play and everybody recognized it. A few of those quatrains were proverbial. *The Rubaiyat* was a very well known poem, as well known in its day as *The Waste Land* got to be, I suppose, and as easily quoted. And it was always there in my head, wanting to come out in some way. James Merrill had used the form of the quatrain in "Lost in Translation" . . .

It's there, isn't it, in the section where the puzzle is being fitted together and the poet is remembering his parents' impending divorce?

When Merrill first saw these, or a large number of them, he said if you go back to the original you realize that so many of Fitzgerald's tend to sag in the middle; you get a string of somewhat undetermined syllables. Merrill's own quatrains are marvelous and compelling. I think also, by the way, and I just now realized this—there's just a slightly earlier poem of mine called "The Mad Potter" (in *Harp Lake*), and in one section of it a bit of *The Rubaiyat* comes back, called the Kuza Nama. I noticed that certain of the lines in "The Mad Potter" really have the Fitzgerald ring in them.

I mentioned Harold Bloom earlier. I know that you've been friends for many years. How has that friendship affected your poetry?

Well, it's a, not a long but a short yet complicated story. I first talked with Bloom with any seriousness in the summer of 1959, although we'd met in Cambridge once or twice before. In 1959 he was already teaching at Yale and I had just gotten my Ph.D. and was coming to teach there. We got to be very close friends very quickly and I had the interesting experience of having as a close friend and joking companion somebody whose literary knowledge overwhelmed me. He had committed more things to memory—that prodigious memory of his—than I could believe, and he knew and appreciated out-of-the-way things, some of which I had thought I had only known myself, and some of which I hadn't known but learned of from him. That is, he represented then nothing of the matter of theory but rather a very old-fashioned, traditional, vast belletristic knowledge, with a tremendously forceful but as yet unrationalized aesthetic agenda (Explanation has never been his long suit.) My first book of poems had just been published, and I realized that he didn't like my poetry very much. He didn't despise it or hate it, but he would say, "Yes, it is very good rhetoric," using Yeats's phrase, meaning "It is well written but not what I mean by poetry." Since that judgment applied to all the work of my contemporaries I admired most, I lived with it, thinking, "That's all right, I have my work to do."

I associate Bloom's point of view with Yeats, as you suggest, but even more with Stevens.

Yes, here was somebody who knew all of Stevens, who promoted him above all others, who brought my attention to those things in Stevens I could not read because I could not read late Stevens, and yet I had so much early Stevens in my head that it kept coming out in all sorts of ways. I had never been able to read "Notes Toward a Supreme Fiction" until talking with Bloom. He said things about Stevens that refocused my entire attention, and

I can't tell you how crucial that was. So yes, Bloom was very important. He was, in those crucial couple of decades, perhaps the best friend and severest critic my poetry had. Not just the critic of my poetry but the friend of it.

And a friend because *of the severity of his criticism.*

Oh, absolutely. More and more and more I encounter young writers of tremendous gifts who've never met anybody who has ever said to them, "Don't do that, it's beneath you." Bloom did this for me, when my teachers had done nothing but encourage me.

Bloom seems to me a moral guide, like Auden telling you not to ruin a fine tenor voice.

Yeah, except that Bloom has nothing to say to anybody about *that* level. It's about something much deeper than that.

That's what I'm wondering. If Auden in some ways gave you the moral sense of his ear for prosody, what was the moral sense Bloom communicated? What was he telling you?

Well, that I had no right not to write mythopoetic poetry. That I had no right simply to write "literature." I could write "literature," most of what he'd read of mine had been "literature," but it was not poetry yet. By which Bloom meant a Longinean, high romantic sense of what poetry is and can do. I think a good rule of thumb for it was what I mentioned earlier—if I wrote a poem that I couldn't understand, maybe it was a real poem.

But what you learned to write was a mythopoetic poetry that came out of, rather than renounced, the lessons of Auden's prosody—

—And not just prosody. I was learning how I could still be concerned with what I had been concerned with and have it get at other things. That Bloom could never understand, and I don't think would ever purport to—that is, the exact way in which the craft of poetry does not stand as a bulwark between yourself and the access to profound fictions or fables or tropes, but provides that access. That is the essential mystery about poetry. There are people who have some myth of access who don't know anything about practice, and there are people who are admired for craft and think that if you have some minor craft of one kind or another that is enough. But the problem is the relation between these things.

I think we've come around to poems that get to be about the world by being about how to talk about it.

Well, put it this way. There used to be earlier on in history, in literary history, an externalized muse. The muse gets more and more and more internalized. What happens when the muse gets internalized in the language itself? When you have to call on that muse in the language, you do it by means of all those technical elements for which meter is only a synecdoche!

Right, "As if the fragments of our speech had spoken."

Yes, in fact, yes. But this is very general and putting it all together requires absolutely detailed concrete instances. That's why I continue to teach.

It seems to me that in its many, tiny parts "Tesserae" is about concrete instances—about living in and through particulars. I mean, your ways of meeting the challenge—and discovering the possibilities—posed by the writing of each quatrain remind me that our thinking, writing, and living are always taking place within particular, concrete circumstances.

"Living through" . . . yes, and this makes me think of an old psychoanalytic phrase, "working through," and the kind of exploration—good painters sometimes call it "searching"—that always comes in poetry. Not just moving from one poem or phase of writing to another, but sometimes within a poem or sequence itself. Some of it entails understanding the possibilities in the cards you've dealt yourself, as well as in acknowledging the ultimate constraints. But without constraints there are no possibilities.

Now, this gets back to my first question about the ethics of writing and its practice, so it may be the right place to stop.

Art is a wonderful model of virtue, for those who contemplate it as much as for those who make it. I am not a musician and I'm not an artist, and yet I learn a tremendous amount about the ability of art to give joy by contemplating works of music and works of visual art. So I can then say I believe this is true for people who are not practitioners of the art of poetry. Art is something that economic or political necessity does not impose on. The late Philip Rahv, the gruff editor of *Partisan Review,* when it was reported to him that somebody had written something or held forth about something, used to say, "Who asked him?" Art occurs when the question can be raised, "Who asked you?" Nobody asked you but Poetry and yourself (Wallace Stevens wrote of "the cry" of the poem's own occasion). Finally, there is the old virtue of craft well-exercised, and of its exemplary force. Having work to do that you can get better and better at, and then make it harder for yourself to get better in *that* way, and to work again on the consequences of that—this is to be fortunate. And you've a moral obligation not to waste your good fortune.